Caroline Kirkland

ALIVE
IN ME

COLOSSIANS

VICTOR MAXWELL

AMBASSADOR

Alive in Me

First published 1994

Copyright © 1994 Victor Maxwell

ISBN   1   898787   11   5

Ambassador Productions Ltd.,
Providence House,
16 Hillview Avenue,
Belfast, BT5 6JR

INTRODUCTION

The Christian life is not easy. It never was. Believers in the city of Colosse during the first century did not find it easy, nor do you on your Main Street today. Persecution and prejudice threatened their existence. In a pagan society they felt vulnerable and exposed to false teachers who sought to waylay them from the simplicity of the gospel and the sufficiency of Jesus Christ.

Hearing of their need for affirmation in their Christian faith and the application of Christ's Gospel to their daily lives, the great Apostle Paul, from a prison cell, wrote them a letter to encourage them in the faith. In this letter he addressed issues and heresies with which those first century Christians wrestled. To encounter false teachers with their deceptive philosophies, Paul set forth the absolute supremacy and sufficiency of Jesus Christ in every situation. Paul declares, "In Him dwells all the fullness of the Godhead bodily" and then adds, "and you are complete in Him." 2:9,10) Jesus Christ is fully God and Christians being in Him have everything they need.

Paul further enlightened them that not only were they in Christ, but Jesus Christ is alive in the Christian.(1:27) Motivated by the Christian's sufficiency in Jesus Christ, Paul exhorted the Colossian believers to let Christ live out His life in them, in their homes, on their streets and in the workshops of Colosse. Jesus Christ was exactly Who they needed, He was everything they needed and He was the only One they needed. He is fully adequate in us and for us today.

The story is told of the celebrated German sculptor J.H. von Dannecker that when he was asked by Napoleon Bonaparte to make a statute of Venus for the gallery of the Louvre he refused. The emperor then offered the sculptor an enormous sum of money but he still turned down the request. Napoleon was angry and demanded to know the reason why. Dannecker answered, "Sir, I have made a statute of Jesus Christ and I can never use my chisel to carve an inferior subject." When we have Christ all else is inferior to Him. He has no rivals.

Paul, in his letter, used his pen to set forth Jesus Christ as the One Who in all things must have all preeminence. That letter has been preserved for us through the centuries and is included in the Bible as the Epistle of Paul to the Colossians. It was just the word that was needed in Colosse at that time.

Perhaps you too feel assailed by misunderstandings, criticism and prejudices. Maybe your Christian life and faith are on trial in your neighbourhood or work place. What was good to give the Colossians that thrust of encouragement in their hard times, may be just what the Great Physician would order for your Christian life in your difficult stretch. You may find yourself singing Charles Wesley's famous hymn:

Thou O Christ art all I want,
More than all in Thee I find.

This book is the outcome of a series of studies conducted at Templemore Hall, Belfast, on Monday evenings. During the series I drew widely from many writers and commentators both modern and old. Their writings have not only greatly helped and blessed me, but also permeate this simple commentary. That is my disclaimer to plagiarism! Just as you would not eat all a week's rations at one go so these studies are not meant to be read at one go nor in isolation. I invite you to accompany your reading of each study with the Bible and add your own thoughts and comments. Also, study in itself is futile unless we are prepared to implement the knowledge God gives us. Having studied the Word, step out and put it into your shoe leather.

I am grateful to the patient and encouraging church family at Templemore Hall to whom I have had the joy of ministering God's Word. I am also thankful to my own family for their constant support and keeping me in touch with reality! Tomm Knutson, my son-in-law, helped me with the manuscript and he knows how much this is appreciated.

Victor Maxwell

*V*ictor and Audrey Maxwell have been
associated with Acre Gospel Mission for
almost thirty years. About half of that time
was invested serving the Lord in a pioneer
and church planting ministry in the Amazon
jungles of Brazil. The balance of the years
have been employed in pastoral and
evangelistic ministry in United Kingdom
and United States of America. This book is
the outcome of a series of Monday evening
Bible Studies conducted in Templemore
Hall where Victor has pastored the church
for almost nine years.

1

"THE EPISTLE AND THE APOSTLE"

COLOSSIANS 1:1,2

When Andrew Morton released his book, "My Story," detailing the life of Diana, the Princess of Wales, he burst a bubble that left many people disappointed and disillusioned with life behind the closed doors of the royal residences at Kensington Palace and Highgrove. On the heels of Mr. Morton's sensational publication came the equally sensational revelations about Sarah, the Duchess of York, and the consequent breakdown of her royal marriage. Faith in royalty and esteem for the Royal family had been dealt a heavy blow.

Margaret Thatcher's book "The Downing Street Years" was soon on the book shelves. In this book Baroness Thatcher, in her own and inimitable and forthright manner, spilled the beans by frankly telling of the treachery and double dealing that went on within her Cabinet, and at times behind her back, prior to her forced resignation after eleven years at the top of British politics. Once again the Cabinet revelations left many disillusioned and disappointed with some of our political leaders.

Nor has the Church escaped the public's disenchantment with organised religion. The notorious Bishop of Durham has relegated the Christmas message to a matter of myth and fable, and other clerics readily agree. Thanks to this confusion brought on by those who profess to belong to Christendom, the same disappointments and frustrations have also effected some people's perception of Jesus Christ.

Too many voices tell us that we need something more than Jesus Christ - some more-exciting experience. Others propose that we can do with something less than Jesus Christ saying all ways lead to one God. And many preach something, or someone, other than Jesus Christ. Sadly, amongst many Christians a mild indifference to the centrality and supremacy of our Blessed Lord Jesus Christ has set in.

Our purpose in this study is to return to the trustworthy pages of Holy Scripture so that we can have a fresh appreciation of Who Jesus Christ really is, what place He occupies and how relevant He is to our times. It is too easy to become jaded and faded in our appreciation of our Saviour.

Paul's letter to the Colossians, four short chapters that require about twenty minutes reading, sets before us the fulness of Christ and our completeness in Him. This epistle also makes the living Christ relevant to Christian living. Even as we study this short book we will find that it is a mine of spiritual truth with inexhaustible treasures for the reader and for all who study its sacred pages.

It is good to remember that twenty of the New Testament books were written as letters. This fact underlines the importance and impact of good correspondence. There are many people who may not be good at public speaking, but are good communicators when it comes to writing. When I recall this, I sometimes think I should have loved to have been there when some of these letters were written. They were dictated by Paul; however, we remember that many of the letters were written while Paul was in prison so maybe we wouldn't have been too comfortable with him there. We may therefore dream of being for when the letter was read in the church.

When you read this letter try to imagine being in Colosse for the first reading. Maybe at times that would have been uncomfortable too! Paul had some very pointed things to say about the Christian and his home, the Christian at his work and the Christian in the church. Apart from stating the pre-eminence of Christ, Paul also has instruction for practical every-day Christian living in a pagan society.

1. CORRESPONDENT - PAUL

Paul is one of those people so admired by Christians that sometimes he seems larger than life. Apart from the Lord Jesus, no other person in the New Testament looms so tall as the Apostle Paul. His pedigree is impressive even before his conversion. (See Phil 3:3-6) On the Damascus Road he was struck blind, and then after his conversion he was lifted to incredible heights as an apostle, evangelist, pastor, missionary and finally a martyr.

No one was more committed to the cause of Christ than Paul. He penned thirteen of the twenty letters of the New Testament and planted churches throughout the Roman Empire. On the occasion of writing this letter, and that of Galatians, Ephesians, and Philipians, he is in jail, and he writes to the saints in Colosse even though he has never visited that city. (1:4,9,2:1)

2. COLOSSE - THE PLACE

Colosse was one of a trio of cities, Laodicea and Hieraplois being the other two. It was situated about 125 miles S.E. from the coastal city of Ephesus. The area was rich in minerals, and these cities formed a sort of common market and were very prosperous. The large population reflected the cosmopolitan nature of the Roman world. Greek philosophies abounded, and many religious zealots expounded all sorts of heresies. The loose living of the Romans was endemic. There was also a large Jewish colony and a synagogue in the city.

3. CHURCH - THE PEOPLE

Colosse doesn't exist today, and we would not be speaking of the it except for the fact that there was a church in that place. The most important thing happening in the world today is what God is doing in the Church.

Neither the city of Colosse nor the Church in that city are mentioned in the book of Acts. However, during Paul's three year ministry in Ephesus there was an outgrowth of the work which obviously reached into colosse, Heirapolis and Laodacia. So effective was the witness and so great was that growth that "all which dwelt in Asia heard the word...both Jews and Greeks."

One of Paul's converts in Ephesus was Epaphras, who was a native of Colosse. He took the message back home, and through his witness the church was founded. (1:4-7; 4:12-13) Philemon was probably a convert of Paul's as well, and it seems that he and his family opened their home for the church meeting. The membership of this young church was largely made up of Gentiles.

4. CONDITION - THE PROBLEM

Paul, as a prisoner in Rome, received a visit from Epaphras who reported to him how new teaching had infiltrated the church and was threatening to destroy the whole ministry of the church. What was this heresy? It was a heresy that denied the supremacy and sufficiency of Jesus Christ as Head of the Body, His Church.

The heresy was commonly called Gnosticism, which was a combination of eastern mysticism and Jewish legalism. The Gnostics regarded all matter as evil. Because matter was evil, God could not have created evil matter. They therefore introduced the teaching of angels as emanations from God. These angels were said to create matter without God being contaminated. This gave rise to a form of Pantheism whereby God was removed from His creation. They also held to a form of astrology and reading of the skies to foretell the future.

Such teaching undermined the foundation of the Christian faith. First, it attacked the Person of Christ. Gnostics considered Christ to be just another of God's emanations and relegated Him to the bottom of the tier. They further attacked the Sufficiency of Jesus Christ ; all of this attacked the Supremacy of Jesus Christ. They also taught that because the body was evil there was a different and divergent view of ethics. Some offered that the body should be subdued to an aesthetic life style. Others felt the contrary. They taught that, because the body was evil, they could indulge in sensuality and all forms of immoral abuse.

Added to these were the narrow views of Jewish ritualism, circumcision, dietary laws, feasts, fasting and holy days. In effect, all of these combined as enemies of the Church of

Christ and of the Christ of the Church. Hence Paul sounds the alarm, "Beware..." (2:8)

5. CONTENT - THE PURPOSE

Paul's letter to the Ephesians was written about the same time and maybe delivered on the same journey by Onesimus and Tychicus. There are many similarities in the letters. In the letter to the Ephesians the emphasis is on the Church as the Body and Christ as the Head; in the letter to the Colossians the emphasis is on Christ as the Head of Body; in Ephesians the believer is " in Christ in the heavenlies;" (Eph. 1:3) in Colossians Christ is " in the believer on earth." (Col.1:27) Paul used the same vocabulary that the Gnostics used but gave deeper and fuller meaning to the language. Words such as "perfect", "complete" and "fulness" were employed by the apostle. He also had a lot to say about wisdom, knowledge, understanding, angels and spirit powers. However, the main thrust of the letter is the Pre-eminence of Jesus Christ; we need no angels to mediate for us;

Christ is sufficient. "In Him dwells all the fulness of the Godhead bodily...and we are complete in Him."

(a) The Truth about Christ is Defined.
(1:1-29)

It is important to note that Paul did not begin by attacking the heretics. First, he began by encouraging the saints in his introduction. He assured them of his love and prayers for them. He then proceeded to exalt the Saviour and set forth the

The Deity of Jesus Christ. (1:1-19)
The Death of Jesus Christ. (1:20-22)
The Demands of Jesus Christ. (1:23-29)

(b) The Truth About Christ is Defended. (2:1-23)

The life we are to experience. (2:1-7)
The lies we are to expose. (2:8-23)

(c) The Truth about Christ is Demonstrated. (3:1-4:1)

Purity in the heart. (3:1-11)
Fellowship in the Church.   (3:12-17)
Harmony in the home.   (3:18-21)
Diligence in our work.   (3:22-4:1)

(d) The Truth about Christ is Declared. (4:2-18)

Faithfulness in our witness. (4:2-6)
Love in our Service.   (4:7-18)

In an age of syncretistic worship as we have today, we need to study and proclaim the book of Colossians.

2

"TO THE CHRISTIANS IN COLOSSE WITH LOVE"

COLOSSIANS 1:1-8

Fifty years ago France was occupied by the Nazi forces of Adolf Hitler. During that occupation there were many brave men and women of the French Resistance who were out to frustrate and eventually help defeat their enemy. In the first days of the Nazi invasion many of these resistance volunteers removed all the road signs in France so that the advancing German army did not know which way to turn or what direction to take. It led to a lot of confusion and frustration.

I sometimes feel that the frustration and confusion of our times is because the "sign posts" have been taken down. In France it was done to frustrate the enemy, but now it would seem it is the enemy who has removed the signposts. There are many in our troubled Province who just do not know which way to turn or what direction to take. In such a time of crisis we need to turn back to the Holy Scriptures. In God's Word alone we find the only reliable signpost for living. We need to get back to the Bible.

In the pagan world of the first century there was much confusion invading the Church. In his letter Paul was giving sign posts to the church in Colosse to point them in the right direction and seeking to focus them on Christ.

In the first chapter Paul sets about exhorting the saints, exalting the Saviour and explaining his service for Christ. In other words, he is uplifting the saints, uplifting the Saviour and uplifting his Christian service.

1. PAUL'S EXHORTATION TO THE SAINTS (1:1-12)

(a) Greetings to the Church (vs. 1,2)

Paul does two things in this initial greeting. First he gives identification of who he is and then a salutation to the church in Colosse. When the Colossians broke the seal on this letter, the first word they would have read was "Paul." Think of the impact of that name upon them. He was to the early church what Martin Luther was to the German Christians of reformation times. The Colossians must have been stirred and encouraged to receive a letter from the great apostle.

Paul tenderly establishes his authority to them - he is an apostle of Jesus Christ. He further indicates his allegiance to the will of God and further proceeds to display his affection for the saints.

Alongside Paul's name is that of Timothy, who not only must have been recognised but also greatly respected by the saints. Who could ever forget young Timothy who was Paul's constant companion and fellow worker in Asia? While Paul ministered in Ephesus, perhaps Timothy travelled with others throughout the region preaching the Word. It is also likely that during this period he even visited Colosse.

In Paul's salutation to the church, note how he describes them as "saints." Remember these were discouraged believers in Colosse, and although Paul had never met them, his words must have been dynamic. The term "saints" is drenched with meaning. It simply means "set apart to be holy." Although this term has more to do with position than condition, it is important that we seek to be what God says we are. (See Jas. 2:17) We should live worthily of the name He has given us.

"Faithful brethren in Christ Jesus."   These "faithful brethren" were not an elite group amongst the church members. Rather this title was relative to every believing brother and sister in Christ. The saints were physically "in Colosse" but spiritually "in Christ." Just as a letter in a bottle is in the ocean - the letter is in the water but, the letter is also in the bottle and untouched by the water. So are we in the world but also "in Christ." Christ in us is the hope of glory. (1:27;) "Us" in Christ is the hope of our security.

Following his indication of the Christian's position "in Christ...in Colosse," Paul then says, "Grace be to you..." In Christ there is grace to live in Colosse. There is always grace to abound unto every good work in every place that God has put us. Replace the name of Colosse with the place where you live or work. There is grace to live in that place as a faithful brother or sister in Christ.

It is interesting how Paul throughout this letter takes common words and gives them a deeper and fuller meaning as they relate to believers in Christ. That is what he does with his greeting to the Church where both Jew and Gentile believers worshipped together.

"Grace" was the word commonly used by Gentile Greeks in their salutation. It speaks of the joy and favour which comes to us from God our Father and the Lord Jesus Christ. Grace is not just God's unmerited favour. Grace is God giving us what we do not deserve; when we were against merit and favour, enemies and rebels, He was still gracious to us. Grace is God giving us what we do not deserve. John Newtown wrote:

In evil long I took delight
Unmoved by shame or fear.
Till a new object struck my sight
And stopped my wild career.

Amazing grace how sweet the sound
That saved a wretch like me.

"Peace" was the Jewish greeting. It is important to note the order - - peace follows after grace. Peace comes only when, through g race, we are rightly related to Jesus Christ. Grace and peace are what the saints in Colosse needed. God can make grace abound to us in every place and give us peace in any place.

(b) Gratitude for the Church (vs. 3-5)

"We give thanks to God..." Thanksgiving is a lost art amongst many of the Lord's people today. We take so much for granted, and our carnal attitude toward things can make us to be grumblers. Picture Paul listening to Epaphras relate to him all about the church in Colosse. Having heard it all, he turns to Timothy and Epaphras and says "Let's first of all give thanks." It is a great exercise to positively focus on the things for which we are to be grateful. (See 1 Thess. 5:18; Eph. 5:4, 15-20; Phil 4:6) We need to serve our apprenticeship at thanksgiving. Thanksgiving is an essential part of a balanced prayer life. Alongside Paul's thanks giving were also his prayers. When he heard of their needs he turned those needs into prayers.

(c) Grace in the Church (vs. 6)

We are given an insight to what Paul heard as he listened to Epaphras. He doubtless heard of their problems, but he also heard of their faith, love and hope. It is noteworthy that Paul was able to trace the grace of God in their lives.

Thanksgiving gives us a positive attitude towards others. It looks for good in others, for grace in others. In this grace we seek to underline the marks and traits of a full Christian life - faith, hope and love. Thirteen times in Paul's writings do we come across this little triplet of "faith, hope and love." We shall see how these words indicate the whole history of a believer.

Faith began in the past - Faith in the Saviour. It is not surprising that faith is always mentioned first in this trio. That is where the Christian life begins - the step of faith in Christ. We also continue by faith - the walk of faith. Faith will only cease when we see Christ. Love operates in the present - Love for all the saints. Faith proves its reality by expressing itself through love. We know we have faith in God and love for God when we love the saints. It is a wonderful thing when one sees in the church love for all the saints - not just for some, not just for friends, not just for the lovable, but for all the saints. Here in Colosse there was love from the youngest to the oldest, the immature and the mature, the leaders and the followers.

It is worth noting that verse eight is the only time the "Spirit" is mentioned in Colossians, and it is mentioned in relation to love. Only the Holy Spirit gives us love for all the saints. We are commanded to love all the saints and because we ought, we can, and because we can, we must.

Hope looks to the future - The hope of salvation. Verse five should read as "through the hope which is laid up for you..." or "because of the hope..." This hope is not that of star gazing, but rather is a living hope that motivates love and strengthens faith. These Colossians had been pagans, "without God and without hope in the world." When they received the Word of God by faith, they then had hope.

What began with faith is preserved by hope, encouraged by hope and revitalized by hope. Because we have hope, faith is strong, and our love is constant. The hope of glory and our heavenly reward should make a difference in how we live. (Titus 2:11-13; 1John 3: 2,3)

(d) Great Servant of the Church (vs. 7,8)

Paul was a Christian gentleman. He was always unstinted in his praise of others. Here he encourages them by eulogizing Epaphras. Paul saw him as:
A Fellow servant (Phil.23
A Faithful servant (Col.1:7) A Fervent servant (Col.4:12)

What greater tribute can be said of a man than what Paul said of Epaphras - "a faithful minister of Christ." Paul refers to the reach of this man's work - "the Gospel came unto you", and also the results of this man's work - "and brings forth fruit."

(e) Growth in the Church (vs.9-12)

Paul in his introduction assures the Colossians of his prayers. Here he actually engages in prayer because of the things he has heard. One of the secrets of Paul's ministry was his prayer life. Preaching and praying were two dynamic means of grace which Paul exercised in all his ministry. It is also to be noted that Paul was in prison, and yet he was praying for others! Paul has so much to teach us.

Paul's prayer will be the subject of our next study.

3

"PAUL IS PRAYING FOR US"

COLOSSIANS 1:8-12

On January 13, 1969, James and Dorrie Gunning, two missionaries in Brazil with Acre Gospel Mission, were travelling in a Brazilian Air Force plane that was lost at night time over the Amazonian jungle. The crew and passengers had almost given up any hope of survival. In the midst of such despair James read to Dorrie the "Daily Light" for that day and claimed God's promises given in the reading, "Cast thy burden on the Lord and He will sustain you. He shall not suffer the righteous to be moved."

Miraculously they were found by another Air Force plane sent out to search for the lost plane. With only twenty minutes fuel left in the plane's tanks, they landed on an airfield where car headlights lit up the runway. When they returned to Northern Ireland two years later and recounted this story of God's protection, they discovered that a group of people had met to pray for them on that very date.

When Mollie Harvey, a colleague of James and Dorrie Gunning in Brazil, was attacked by an Indian who tried to assault her, she was wonderfully delivered from his evil intentions. She also traced that on that very night people had been praying for her. Such incidents as these have happened many times and affirm the power and effect of intercessory prayer.

In the final scene from Tennyson's "Idylls of the King," King Arthur, from his death bed, speaks to a friend those familiar words, " Pray for my soul. More things are wrought by prayer than this world dreams of." Edith Schaeffer said, "Prayer is as natural as breathing and more necessary than oxygen." How true this is. Through prayer we are drawn into the arena where heaven and earth border, to the very gate of heaven and to the Throne of Grace. Prayer is the voice of faith.

Some of the richest portions of Paul's writings are those containing his prayers for the saints. Paul was a man of prayer. The testimony that flowed from his pen is evidence that he not only believed in prayer, he prayed! His Christian life got started with prayer (Acts.9:10-11). He prayed for himself (2Cor.12:7-9), and requested that others pray for him (Eph.6:18-20; 2Thess. 3:1). Likewise, he also engaged in intercessory prayer for others (2 Thess.1:11).

Paul in his introduction assures the Colossians of his prayers.(v.3) In verse nine he actually engaged in prayer because of the things he had heard. One of the secrets of Paul's ministry was his prayer life, and what a mighty prayer this is. We should also remember that although Paul was in prison and he was praying for others.

In a previous study I suggested using our thoughts of being in Colosse when the Apostle wrote to the Christians there. Try to probe the reasons why he wrote what he did. If Paul were to write us a letter what would be the issues he would raise with the saints a t in our church? Good question! If, after hearing our problems and circumstances, we could join him as he prayed for the us, I think we would find that his prayer for the Colossians would not differ much from what he would pray for the Christians in our church. Paul's prayer is a model prayer of how we should pray for our churches and for ourselves.

It should be of particular interest and relevance to us all in our materialistic age, to note that when Paul prayed, he primarily prayed for the spiritual welfare of the saints rather than their physical well-being or material prosperity. It is not wrong to pray for the physical and material needs of God's people, but their spiritual state is more important.

1. PAUL'S PRAYING WAS DEDICATED

The urgency in his prayer. "From the time we heard..." As soon as Epaphras related to Paul the condition of the church, Paul translated that news into prayer. Can it be that we have failed in a sense of urgency before God when we hear about the troubles a round us? Remember Nehemiah viewed Jerusalem and turned his heartbreak into tearful intercession. Nehemiah cared for Israel and Jerusalem and prayed for them urgently. (Acts 12:5) The urgent need of the church is not just for prayer but also for pray-ers - people who will pray.

The persistency in his prayer. "Do not cease to pray for you." This is the principle taught by our Lord when He said, "Men ought always to pray and not to faint." Luke 18:1. Paul also taught the new Christians "to pray without ceasing..." 1 Thess.5:17 Too soon we give up in our praying. Later in this letter Paul tells the Colossians to "continue in prayer."(Col.3:6) Paul was not a quitter.

Bobby Irvine was my very good friend. For fifty years his wife prayed that he would come back to the Lord. I was there in the hospital to see that prayer answered. Thank God Olive and her family were not quitters.

The unity in his prayer. In his prayer he includes his present company by use of the pronoun "we..." To pray alone is taught by Jesus Christ.(Mt. 6:6) But we are also taught to come together to pray. (Acts.1:12-14; 16:5; 12:5; 13:1-3) Remember, even our Lord took company with Him to the Garden of Gethsemene when He went to pray.

2. PAUL'S PRAYING WAS FULL OF DESIRE

"For you." Here Paul indicates his intensity in prayer. He opens his heart to God for the Colossian Christians even though he had never seen them. We can do no better for our friends than to pray for them. Prayer builds bridges between us and God and between us and the saints. Paul's passionate love for the saints led him to pray for them. (Mt.17:21; and 1 Kings. 17:17-21)

3. PAUL'S PRAYING WAS DEFINITE

Note the re-occurrence of the little word "all" - "all wisdom... all pleasing... all might... all patience." He was desirous that these believers be complete in their Christian experience. Hence he prayed that they might know:

(a) Wisdom of the will of God. (v.9)

Words such as "knowledge, wisdom and spiritual understanding" were part of the gnostics vocabulary. Unashamed,

Paul takes these words and uses them in his prayer for the Church. These terms were deceitfully usurped by the enemies of Christ. "In Jesus Christ are hidden all the riches of wisdom and knowledge." The Christian is to grow in the knowledge and grace of the Lord Jesu s.(2Pet.3:18)

The word "filled" means to be controlled, or be to completed. It is the word that was used for a ship that was rigged, stored and ready to sail. The gnostics agreed that the knowledge of Jesus Christ was a good beginning But they believed progress on wisdom could only be made by the multitude of philosophies that they held to, and the observance of holy days and practice of rituals and astrology. This was an attack on the sufficiency of the Saviour. Paul met this false teaching head on and prayed that the Christians might have their knowledge completed in Christ. This completeness and sufficiency of the Christian in Jesus Christ is repeated throughout the letter.

The word knowledge which Paul uses here, has to do with a growing understanding of the vital truths of our faith; however, this knowledge must be held in spiritual wisdom. That is, allowing the knowledge of God in His Word to condition our spiritual understanding and govern our practical living. For the Apostle, a deep growing knowledge of Jesus Christ and of His Word is of the utmost importance to the spiritual development of all Christians.

It is vital for spiritual growth for the Christian to know, to do and to prove the will of God. (Eph.5:17-18 and Rom.12:1,2) The Scriptures are the primary source of knowledge for the believer, and as they are studied under the guidance of the Holy Spirit, they condition the understanding and mind of the believer.

(b) A worthy walk with God. (v.10)

After "acquaintance with the will of God," there should follow "obedience to the will of God." There should always be a solidarity between what we know and how we behave. What we learn should teach us how to live.

D. L. Moody said, "Every Bible should be bound in shoe leather." Paul prays that they may "walk worthy to all pleasing." The Christian's highest aim is to please the Lord.

Throughout his New Testament letters Paul reminded believers to "walk worthy of our calling" (Eph.4:1), "worthy of the Gospel" (Phil 1:27), and "worthy of the Kingdom" (2 Thess. 1:5). Our highest motive is to walk worthy of the Lord, of His teaching, of His example, of His Cross, and of His promised return.

(c) A worthwhile work for God. (v.10)

"Fruitful in every good work." The result of a walk worthy of the Lord is a worthwhile work for Him; a devoted life will produce diligent service for Christ. Before we came to know the Lord, our lives were unprofitable and unfruitful. This was illustrated f or the Colossians in Onesimus, the run-away slave who after a wasted life found forgiveness in Jesus Christ. (Philemon 10-11)

God works in us to bear fruit through us. (John 15:16) Fruit-bearing is the result of the life of Christ in us. There are three stages of this fruit-bearing: "fruit" (John 15:2), "more fruit" (15:5), "much fruit" (15:8). Paul's use of the present continuous participle, "being fruitful," means he prayed that their fruit-bearing would be constant and ongoing. To be constantly producing fruit we need to constantly abiding in Christ. (2Tim.4:11; Acts. 13:13)

(d) A wealthy experience of God. (v.11)

"Increasing in the knowledge of God." Again this is in the present continuous mood. As we do the will and work of God, we increase in the knowledge of Him.

"Strengthened by the might of God." Flowing out of the strength and power that God gives there is "patience, endurance and joy". These follow one from another. (Daniel 11:32) Endurance is what the Colossian Christians needed as they faced formidable forces of evil in their city. Abraham needed endurance when he walked as a pilgrim through a strange land. Moses needed endurance when armed with the promises of God he came up against an obstinate Pharaoh. Christians today should face trials with endurance, perseverance and steadfastness. This only comes in our experience through the outworking of His mighty power in our lives.

Patience follows from endurance. Patience is strength under pressure and this leads to joy when we know God and are strengthened by Him. How we all need to pray for these virtues in our lives.

(e) A whole hearted worship of God. (v.12)

"Giving thanks..." Already we have seen that the Christian should be thankful and positive. (Eph.5:18-20) Thanksgiving keeps us sweet, but when we lose our joy we become sour grumblers. Here Paul reminds us that we should be grateful for our inheritance, our deliverance and our forgiveness. Let us refuse to be like the nine leprous men who did not return to give thanks to the One who had healed them.

Interceding for other Christians is one of the most effective ministries we can engage in. Ask James and Dorrie Gunning or Mollie Harvey about the times someone prayed for them when they were eye-ball to eye-ball with danger. When God calls His people to pray and they obey, things begin to happen. Why not pray for someone just now? Incidently, another promise from "Daily Light" for January 13 is, "I will trust, and not be afraid: for the Lord Jehovah is my strength and my song; He also is become my salvation."

4

"WHO IS JESUS CHRIST?"

COLOSSIANS 1:13-29

All the major religions of the world are dominated by great leaders or great teachers. In Buddhism there is Siddharta Gautama, known as the Buddha. The founder of Islam is Muhammed. Judaism reveres Moses as their prophet. However, while all of these men are representative of their religions none of them are indispensable to their religions. Their teachings can stand alone apart from the personalities.

Christianity is altogether different. Christianity is Christ. His person and work are the rock upon which the Christian faith is built. If He is not Who He said He was, and if He did not do what He came to do, then the foundation of Christianity is undermined and the whole structure of Christianity must collapse. Take Christ from Christianity, and we are left with nothing. Christ is the heart and centre of Christianity. The question then may be asked, "Who is Jesus Christ?" The pages of history are replete with various answers to this question. Some would relegate Him to being a mere man, others would say He is one of many gods, while yet others hold that He was God manifested in human form.

Concepts of who Jesus Christ was were just as varied in the first century and nowhere more so than in Colosse. Gnostics, Jews and mystics combined in relegating Jesus Christ to some one less than God and undervalued the sufficiency of Jesus Christ as the solitary Saviour. Not only did they attempt to rob Christ of His essential deity, but in doing so, they sought to destroy the whole base and foundation of the Christian faith.

It was on hearing of this attack on Christianity and Christ that Paul took pen in hand, not only to encourage the Christians in Colosse, but also to exalt Christ in His rightful preeminent place in the midst of such fierce onslaughts from a pagan world.

Note the three tiers of truth that follow through the rest of this chapter, each one built upon another. First, Paul defends the deity of Jesus Christ by the names ascribed to Him. These names set forth Christ as the Sum and Centre of all things. Because of Who Jesus Christ is, then what He has done for us is of infinite and eternal worth. Flowing freely to us in Christ there follows deliverance from the power of darkness, redemption from the slave market of sin, forgiveness and free pardon of our guilt and sin and the kiss of reconciliation as we are brought into the family of God.

PAUL DEFENDS THE DIETY OF CHRIST BY NAMING WHO HE IS

There is a great day coming when Jesus Christ will have the preeminence, a day when He will be confessed as Lord. However, Paul asserts the preeminence of Jesus Christ (1:18). Jesus Christ has the preeminence because He is:

(a) The Son of His Love. (v.13)

"...the Son whom God loves." This term flows out of "thanks to the Father.." This term gives us an insight into the love of God. His Kingdom is a kingdom of love. The love of God is supremely manifested in Jesus Christ. (Mt.3:17; 17:5; John 17:24; Eph.1:4) How greatly God must have loved us to sacrifice the Son Whom He loves. From this title there issues a composite picture of the preeminent Christ without His name being mentioned.

(b) The Image of the Invisible. (v.15)

The word "image" is the Greek word "eikon" from which we derive our English word "icon". It means a precise copy, an exact reproduction. To call Christ the "Eikon of God" means that He is the exact reproduction of God and revelation of God. John also uses similar language in saying that Jesus Christ is the Word. This means that He is the identical thought and exact expression of God.

Jesus Christ is God in substance, and all that God is, Christ is. This is the thought the writer to the Hebrews expressed when he declared that Jesus Christ was "the brightness of His glory and the express image of His person."(Heb. 1:3) This express image is the imprint left by a seal or die on wax. Hence Jesus Christ exactly mirrors God because in very essence He is God.

This declaration about Jesus Christ cut across all the gnostic teaching of angels emanating from God and a God who is removed and cannot be known.

(c) The Firstborn of every creature. (v.15)

It is here that we come to the eye of the storm that has raged around Christology since the days of the Nicean Council of 325 A.D. Many mistakenly take this term to infer that Jesus Christ was a creature rather than Creator. It is on this error that many of the "isms" flounder. This is a favourite text for the Jehovah Witnesses who characteristically wrest the Scriptures and try by this verse to teach us that Jesus Christ is a created being. They ignore the principle of comparing Scripture with Scripture. The following verse 16 tells us that Jesus Christ is the Creator and not a creature.

Heretics of old taught that Jesus Christ was a created being of higher status than angels but neither eternal nor divine. This was the heresy exposed at the famous Council of Nicea for which Arius was excommunicated. The term "first born" should be considered as a position of priority rather than a period of time. The term simply means "of first importance, of first rank." "First" is the superlative of "before" in that He is absolute first. Nothing ever came before Him in time or order. None is above Him in dignity, importance nor honour.

"Born", speaks of His eternal generation, proceeding from the Father.(Psalm 89:27) Jesus Christ is the highest of the high - the Son of the Highest. He is preeminent above all creation for He is Creator.

(d) The Creator of all things. (v.16)

"For by Him were created all things..." This phrase is reflective on the previous statement of Him being the "first born" for He is the Creator of all things. Ability to create belongs to God alone. In creation He made all things to exist, both things material and things spiritual, the visible and the invisible, authorities and potentates. Warren Wiersbe says, "Jesus Christ is the Sphere in which all things exist, the Agent by which they came into being and the One for Whom all things were made." In time He was before all things, and as He originated all things, so also He holds all things together. (v.17 Heb.1:3) Note the repetition of "all things" six times.

(e) The Head of the Church (v.18)

Having affirmed Christ's relationship to the Father as the Son of His love and the Image of God (vs.13,15) and His relationship to creation in that He is Creator and Sustainer of all things, Paul now sets forth Christ's relationship to the Church. "He is the head of the body..." The word "head" gives the sense of origin and source as well as leader and ruler.

Of all the images given of the Church the most profound is that of the body. The Body is not limited to one assembly but rather takes in the whole family of God in heaven and on earth and of that Body, the Church, Christ is the Head. He is both the Source and Leader of the Church, and just as the body is controlled by the head, so Christ is in control of His Body, the Church.

Also, in the Church Jesus Christ is the beginning - the Sovereign, "The Firstborn from the dead..." Not that He was the first to be raised from the dead. He was not. the Lord Jesus Christ raised Lazarus, a widow's son and Jairus' daughter from the dead. Nevertheless, without His resurrection there could be no resurrection and that would leave Christians, of all men, the most miserable. He is the first fruits of the resurrection. (1Cor. 15:20)

Such preeminence as Paul accords to Jesus Christ, is used in no other place and describes no other person other than

Jesus Christ.(Col.2:9) He alone is worthy to receive the glory, honour and praise ascribed to deity. I remember sharing a room in Jerusalem in 1980 with my good friend George Whitley. Early one morning as the sun was rising over the famous city, George played a cassette on which I was to hear for the first time, a chorus that acclaims the glory and majesty of our blessed Lord; "Majesty." The chorus was written by an American pastor who had been visiting the United Kingdom. As he watched the guards at Buckingham Palace, visited the Tower and viewed the Crown Jewels, he had been struck by the sense of magnificence and majesty of our Royal Family. He was moved to write these words.

Majesty, worship His Majesty;
Unto Jesus be glory, honour and praise.
Majesty, Kingdom authority,
flows from His throne Unto His own, His anthem raise.
So exalt, lift up on high the name of Jesus Magnify,
come glorify, Christ Jesus the King.
Majesty, worship His Majesty Jesus Who died,
now glorified, King of all Kings.

To that we say, "Amen."

5

"HE IS MY EVERYTHING AND MY EVERYTHING IS FOR HIM"

COLOSSIANS 1:13-29

World Mission was the heart motive of Count Nicolaus Ludwig von Zinzendorf in the eighteenth century. When he was sixteen years of age his family had great plans for him to enter upon a diplomatic career. He was sent to study law at the University of Wittenburg. After he qualified he visited Dusseldorf. At the public gallery he was confronted with Stenburg's famous and telling picture of the crucifixion. As he gazed at the masterpiece he was captivated in his soul and challenged by the inscription underneath which read,

"All this I did for thee;
What hast thou done for me?"

Overcome by love for Christ and a deep debt of gratitude, he resolved in his heart to serve the Saviour with all that he had. His life's motto was, "I have but one passion, and that is HE and only HE."

This same Jesus Christ is the prevailing theme of Colossians chapter one. Flowing from Who He is, comes the work He has done for us , and flowing out of the work He has done for us, is the debt we owe to Him.

Already we have been looking at the awesome majesty of our blessed Saviour as we have beheld it in the wondrous names by which He is called. Each name sets forth a facet of glorious truth about the wonderful person of our blessed Lord. The whole passage is so full of Christ that it is impossible to deal with all the matters raised. However, issuing from Christ are the blessings of His marvellous grace.

1. PAUL DEFENDS THE DEATH OF CHRIST BY THE WORK HE DID

Because of Who He is, then what He did is worthy and authentic. What then has He done for His own? There are four words used in these verses that give us different aspects of Christ's great work for us.

(a) Deliverance(v.13)

The word simply means "rescued from danger." It brings us to the battle field. The picture is of a military commander delivering subjugated people out of their captivity and bringing them back into His kingdom of life and liberty. We were the captives held by an alien power - the power of darkness. Jesus Christ is the King Commander Who bruised Satan 's head and set the prisoners free. He has not only delivered us from under the dominion of darkness and bondage of death and sin, He has also translated - transferred - us, into the Kingdom of the Son he loves. He has brought us out of one realm and brought us into His Kingdom emphasizing the power of the Gospel of Jesus Christ.

'Tis the grandest theme, let the tidings roll,
To the guilty heart, to the sinful soul;
Look to God in faith, He will make thee whole:
"Our God is able to deliver thee"

(b) Redemption (v.14)

From the field of battle, Paul now brings us to the market place. The emphasis is not so much on the power of the Gospel, rather it is on the price that Jesus Christ paid for us through His blood. Redemption simply means to "buy back." It is the picture of an offended master in the market who sees the slave who once forsook him. Although the slave is worthy of death for his rebellion, the good master, out of love, is prepared to pay the price to buy him back - to redeem him and let him again enjoy the freedom of the master's family.

We sinners are the slaves sold under sin, bereft of any ability to redeem ourselves. The price is too high, and we are absolutely destitute of merit. Then Christ the Redeemer steps in, and without cause or motive in the slave, He pays the high ransom price - His own blood.(1Tim.2:5)

As there are two aspects in deliverance, so also in redemption. The price Jesus Christ paid made satisfaction to the Father having paid the debt of our sin and suffered our death. That price also brought us merit and procures our title in heaven. In deliverance He brought us out. In redemption He bought us out , and we are not our own.

Free from the Law;
O happy condition!
Jesus has died and there is remission!
Cursed by the Law, and ruined by the Fall,
Grace has redeemed us - once for all!

(c) Forgiveness (v.14)

Now we come to the Supreme Court of Justice where we see the fullness of the pardon purchased for us. The Judge declares us to be guilty and has recorded it so. We are without excuse. When it seems that we should receive what we justly deserve, the Judge declares that our sins have been dealt with by our Substitute Saviour, and on the basis of His atoning death we are now pardoned.

The word forgiveness means "to cancel", or "to send away". That is what Christ did to our sins and debts. He has removed our transgressions from us. On the basis of Christ's death, God has pardoned us; He has sent our sins away, as far as the east is from the west. Now there is nothing found in the records against us. (Rom.8:33,34) The cost of my forgiveness is the blood of Jesus Christ.

To the religions of the world sin is like a running tap that cannot be turned off nor dried up. They do not know how to deal with it much less remove it, but not so with the Christian. The slate has been wiped clean. (1John 1:7,9) He is forgiven and cleansed.

My sin - oh, the bliss of this glorious thought!
My sin - not sin part but the whole,
Is nailed to His cross: and I bear it no more:
Praise the Lord, Praise the Lord, O my soul!

(d) Reconciliation (v.20)

Now we come to a family situation. Once we were estranged and alienated through sin. We were the prodigals in the far country, the sheep lost outside the fold. When Christ died, He not only satisfied divine justice - Jesus Christ through His death has reconciled us to God - He removed the enmity that was between us.(Rom. 3:25; 5:10,11) There is a change of attitude. God is for us, not against us. Where once we were far off, we are now made nigh; once we were strangers, now we are fellow citizens of the household; once we were children of wrath even as others, now we are adopted into the family of God. He has brought us into His banqueting house and His banner over us is love. "God was in Christ reconciling the world unto Himself." (2Cor.5:19)

Reconciliation is the theme of the letter which Paul sent to Philemon, a member of the Colossian church, regarding a runaway slave. Paul pleaded the case for him to be brought back into favour with the master he had offended even though his rebellion was worthy of death. Philemon not only brought him back but also adopted him into the family.

How amazing God's compassion,
That so vile a worm should prove
This stupendous bliss of heaven,
This unmeasured wealth of love!

2. PAUL DEFINES THE DEMANDS OF CHRIST IN WHAT WE OWE

Proceeding out of the delights of His grace which are ours through Christ, Paul now turns to the duties we should render to Him because of Who He is and what He has done. As you read this passage remember that the role of the Christian is a strange one. Some would even accuse us of being weirdos! By human reasoning that is how they see us.

A. W. Tozer said,
"The Christian is an odd number anyway. He feels su-

preme love for One He has never seen, talks familiarly every day with One He cannot see, expects to go to heaven on the virtue of Another, empties himself in order to be full, admits he is wrong so he can be declared right, goes down in order to get up, is strongest when he is weakest, richest when he is poorest, and happiest when he feels worst. He dies so he can live, forsakes in order to have, gives away so he can keep, sees the invisible, hears the inaudible, and knows that which passes all understanding."

We can explain all this by the words of Paul, "the love of Christ constraineth us." (2 Cor. 5:14)

(a) We owe it to Christ to serve Him. (v.23,25)

"I Paul am made a minister." Constantly Paul was proud to call himself "a bond slave of Jesus Christ." He was a servant, a minister, who was sold out to his Master because of love to his Master.(See Exodus 21:1-7) Paul took that same position in relation to Jesus Christ. Stuart Briscoe said, "You cannot be reconciled to God without being recruited for God." How true this is, and there is no service like that of the dedicated Christian who serves out of love for Christ.

(b) We owe it to Christ to suffer for His sake. (v.24)

"Filling up that which is left behind of the afflictions of Christ" This verse presents difficulty to many. It may sound to some as though there was something lacking in the Saviour's atoning suffering and death. Not so. Such a thought would be contrary to what Christ triumphantly cried on the cross, "It is finished." His death procured sufficient and complete atonement for us. The sufferings Paul speaks of here are not those which Christ should have suffered, but rather, those which Paul was appointed to suffer for the cause of Christ.

When God sent Ananias to speak to Paul at the time of his conversion, these words were included, "I will shew him how great things he must suffer for my name's sake."(Acts 9:16) Later Paul wrote to the Philippians, "unto us it is given in the behalf of Christ, not only to believe on Him, but also to suffer for His sake."(Phil. 1:29)

Jesus Christ never promised that the Christian life would be easy. Peter was foretold of the manner of death He would die for Christ.(John 21:17-19) All the apostles, except John, died a martyr's death. Paul reminded Timothy to "endure hardness as a good soldier..."

At Colosse there were certain people who inferred that Paul being in prison brought shame on the Gospel. Paul, rather than being ashamed of his suffering, rejoiced in it because of two things. First, he rejoiced in suffering for the sake of Christ. Paul earnestly desired to know "the fellowship of His sufferings."(Phil.3:10) He was not suffering as an evil-doer or a thief but as one counted worthy to suffer for the Saviour.

Second, he rejoiced in suffering for the sake of the Church. These sufferings were a consequence of his labours for the church and led to the furtherance of the Gospel. (Phil. 1:12)

(c) We owe it to Christ to spread His Word. (vs.27,28)

In verse 23 Paul speaks of the Gospel being preached to "every creature under heaven" and pledged that this was his ministry. It is for that reason he repeats that he preaches "warning every man, teaching every man" and hoping to "present every man." It was this passion that made Paul travel so widely, preach so fervently and serve so faithfully. Mildred Cable, missionary for many years to the people of the Gobi Desert, said, "the greatest crime of the desert was to know where the water was and not to tell others about it." (2 Kings.7:9)

(d) We owe it to Christ to strive in His work. (v.29)

The word "strive" implies strenuous effort like that of an athlete. When Paul associates the word "strive" with "labour," it gives us a picture of the apostle at work - "strenuously labouring." This is the same word he used to the Romans. (Rom. 16:20,30) Yet with all this endeavour, he did not rely on his own strength or power but rather "according to the power that worketh in us mightily." I think it was Spurgeon who said, "Work as though everything depended on you; pray as though everything depended on God." "Christ in us" is not only the hope of glory but also the secret of strength and blessing.

One hundred years ago C.T. Studd played cricket for England and was heir to his father's fortune. However, like Zinzendorf, he was caught up with a passion for Christ and for the lost. He forsook position and wealth to serve God in China, India and the heart of Africa where he died in 1931. He penned these words, "If Jesus Christ be God and died for me, then no sacrifice is too great for me to make for Him."

Can you say, "Amen ?"

6

"AN AGONIZING APOSTLE"

COLOSSIANS 21:1-5

The secular magazines and press are full of "agony aunt" columns, but I often doubt the wisdom, if not the sincerity, of the advice given in them. I remember some years ago when in Korea being asked to translate a letter from Portuguese in which a girl had written seeking counsel. She was asking prayer that her former lover's wife would soon die. This would leave the man free to marry the author of the letter! Enough said!

Paul, from his prison cell in Rome, now gets personal with the Colossian Christians. Like a good shepherd he had a heart for the sheep. Having heard the good news of the saints in Colosse, he now writes a column in which he expresses his concern which he describes as a "conflict." The word used for "conflict" is a word that would have been in familiar use at the various Greek games. "Agon" simply means to wrestle, to struggle or to fight. Paul employed this word in relation to service for Jesus Christ. In 4:1 2; he mentions Epaphras "agonizing," wrestling in prayer for the saints.

Wherever Paul served the Lord there was conflict. The very chains he wore and the cell he occupied were testimony to the intensity of the struggle he had for the church. That he should be in agonizing conflict for saints he had never met tells us a lot about the man and his genuine love for the saints.

At Colosse he is locked in conflict against the heresy of the time, Gnosticism. Paul not only sought as a good shepherd to feed the sheep, but also he fends off the wolves who would devour and destroy the church.

Like modern day cultists, the Gnostics may have been as sincere, as they were self deluding. It was this sincerity and a sense of superiority that made them so beguiling and a threat to the young church in Colosse. They were deceived as to the simplicity, the sufficiency and the superiority of the Christian gospel. Paul takes pen in hand to champion the cause of Christ and set forth the Lord Jesus as the all sufficient Saviour and the believer's completeness in Him.

He therefore states the specific concerns for the church in a personal way, and with that concern he alerts and encourages them in their Christian lives.

1. BE SURE! - A SENSE OF AFFECTION (2:1-3)

Paul, like the Colossians, loved all the saints and was concerned for their welfare. His affection for them brought an agony that was expressed by prayer as well as putting pen to paper(1:9) There is nothing so comforting as to know that others care for us. It is always good to communicate to others that sense of concern and care. What was Paul's concern?

(a) That they be unafraid in adversity.

Paul says that he was concerned that they be comforted. "Comfort" is a compound word which means "with strength" and is better rendered "strengthened" or "encouraged." The name given to the Holy Spirit is "Comforter," the One who puts power into us. He is the "Paraclete," called alongside to put strength into us and encourage us.

You often see a competitor in a race struggling to finish and reach the line. Supporters will get behind him and cheer him on. "Come on, keep going! You can make it." They are putting strength into the competitor. The Holy Spirit comforts us, supports us and puts strength into us in the race we are running.

(b) That they be united in love.

"Knit together in love" This expression is self expressive and a lovely picture of true unity. Love harmoniously compacts and firms brethren together in a bond which transcends barriers of culture and race. This was needed in a church composed of Jews and Gentiles who had been brought into one fellowship in Christ.

Two brothers, one a Christian and the other a member of a fraternal organization, were touring Europe. One day in a European city they encountered a missionary. Immediately the Christian brother and the missionary began an animated conversation on spiritual matters. Later the other brother remarked, "How come you know that fellow?" The Christian replied that he had never met the missionary before. At this the brother exclaimed, "You talked like long lost friends." The Christian brother replied, "More than friends, we are brothers in Christ and belong to the same Lord."

As we are knit together, so shall we be strong. However, it seems in many of our church fellowships we have dropped a stitch or two , and many Christian communities have become unravelled, and we see them torn asunder with division. A motorist stopped and asked a little boy directions to a certain church. The boy innocently replied in a telling way. "Sir, take the road to right, and you will come to two churches. One is the United Church, and the other one is the one you are looking for."

Tertulian wrote that it was said of the early Christians, "How those Christians love each other." They gave a testimony of being knit together in love. Today the world may look on and say, "How they despise each other." Could it be that when we have our true love for Christ we lose our love for each other? Paul likened Christians to a mighty army that does not break rank marching "in order." (2:5) Well did the hymn writer pen the words:

We are not divided,
All one body we,
One in hope and doctrine,
One in charity.

(c) That they be unswerving in faith.

"Unto all riches of full assurance of understanding..." The word used here for assurance is "conviction." Alexander MacLaren wrote, "It was not Erasmus, the polished, learned, scintillating intellect of his time, who made Germany over; it was the rough, rugged Martin Luther with a conviction and compassion as deep as life." Today we again need the assurance and conviction of a Martin Luther. This assurance points to a rich certitude in which there is no doubt or vagueness in doctrine or manner of living.

It is noteworthy that this assurance is linked to being "knit together in love." Love for Christ and for each other, will lead us to a fuller understanding and assurance of the mystery of God which is Jesus Christ. Paul likens this assurance to wealth and prosperity as he piles phrase upon phrase about the fulness there is in Christ. It is the assurance of Who Jesus Christ is and what He has done that makes Christians unashamed.

2. BEWARE! - A SENSE OF ALARM. (2:4,8,16,18)

Whenever you travel abroad you will be aware of notices warning against the possibility of hijackers. Hijacking is endemic to our times. Some hijack planes or ships, others hijack cars and houses. This may be a relatively new phenomena; however, hijacking churches is an old ploy of the Devil. It was happening in Colosse and is still going on today. The Gnostics and other heretics were trying to hijack the church in Colosse and bring the believers into the chains of ritualism and philosophy.

For this reason Paul warns them that they should not be led astray. The seducing false teachers at Colosse presented clever arguments and persuasive words of philosophy and mysticism, of tradition and ritualism, to lead astray the weak and unstable. Spiritual wolves were after the flock of God. (Acts 20:28,29) They would deceive the flock, divide them and then destroy them. To put the church on its guard Paul gave the following warnings:

(a) Beware of Persuasive words.

"...lest any man beguile you with enticing words." (2:4) The Greeks were greatly taken by the use of persuasive speech. Travelling poets and orators attracted large crowds of spectators to hear them articulate with cunning speech on any given subject. The topic chosen was not necessarily a stance that was held by the orator, but with his artful use of words he persuaded the listeners to believe the proposition to be true. Gullible people were duped by the orator.

We should not be surprised to know that the cunning use of words can deceive us. We use rat poison to seduce the rat. Rat poison has more than 95% wholesome content in it. Only the 5% kills! In exactly the same way words were being used by the enemies of the Gospel to destroy the simplicity that is in Christ. The heretics used words that were synonymous with the great words of the Christian faith. The Gnostics changed the meaning and value of the words and used the same language to poison the minds of the believers.

In our age of advanced communicative skills we must beware of those who would employ Christian vocabulary to destroy the Christian faith. Russelites take the name "Jehovah Witnesses," Armstrongism usurps the name "Church of God." These are misrepresentations of Bible truth by using and wresting the Scriptures and thus adulterating Bible language.

Likewise also today, evangelical language is being used to present what is little more than human psychology and much of it under the guise of "counselling." When you have a smooth talker representing flawed teaching to weak minded people, trouble usually follows. Treat such as you would any poison. Get rid of it!

(b) Beware of Worldly Wisdom.

"Beware lest any man spoil you (take you captive) through philosophy and vain deceit. " (Col. 2:8;) It is too easy to be fooled in this life. Paul warned the Colossian Christians lest they get hooked on Godless learning.

Philosophy is the love of wisdom or knowledge. That in itself is not bad, but it should never be used in opposition to God's truth. Milton said, "The end of learning is to know God and out of that learning to love Him and to imitate Him." This concurs with what Solomon said three thousand years ago, "The fear of the Lord is the beginning of wisdom."

The Gnostics of that time loved teaching and learning just for the sake of being educated. Much of the teaching and learning was empty and deceptive. It was linked to the traditions of the various religious strands and formed a sort of syncretism which incorporated the circumcision of the Jews, the fasting of the pagans and rituals of various deities. When one has a knowledge which is devoid of God and handed down tradition which by-passes the authority of God's Word, humanism is the end result.

Humanistic education which leaves God out of the classroom, is like a pilot on a jet plane without navigational aids. He is travelling fast but not sure where he is going. Humanism today in our schools allows the false teaching of evolution and the admission of diverse kinds of worship, and the introduction of situational ethics. Those responsible still do not know where it is all taking us .

(c) Beware of Empty Ritual.

"Let no one judge you in meat, or in drink...." (2:16-18) All men are instinctively religious. In the absence of a knowledge of Gospel truth, they will seek to establish their own religion. For false and counterfeit religion, to have any credibility it must have a guise of what appears to be authentic. No one ever tries to make a counterfeit £19.00 note - it is obvious such a note does not exist. You can only fake a copy of something that is real.

Tradition, ritualism and superstition all smack of modern day Romanism. However, too easily we dismiss our own responsibility in this respect. We also must be careful not to fall into the trap of ritualistic worship in whatever form we adopt.

It is a fact of history that the Gospel triumphed over these false religions and heretical teachings. The various church councils confronted these heresies and false teachers. They affirmed the truth in the great Confessions of Faith which are with us to this day.

Paul taught that the best safeguard against error for the Christian is a full knowledge of Christ and an enthusiastic assurance of His Word. In Col. 2:9 Paul sets forth that the healthy Christian is one who is joined to the living Head and is nourished in the body by the Head, knit together with other believers and increasing in the knowledge of God.

When it comes to heresy always remember that prevention is always better than cure.

7

"THE OLD ACCOUNT WAS SETTLED LONG AGO"

COLOSSIANS 2:6-23

When Longfellow, the poet, was well on in years, his hair was as white as snow, but his complexion was bright and vigorous. An ardent admirer asked the poet how he kept so fresh and how he was able to write so beautifully. To this the poet replied pointing to an apple tree, "That tree is very old but its blossoms are now prettier than they have ever been and that is because it grows a little new wood every year. Like the apple tree, I too try to grow a little new wood every year." And so he did.

"Grow up!" Have you ever heard that said? Have you ever had to say it? Sometimes these words are uttered in disgust by an older person, sometimes in jest by a friend; other times they are the outburst of frustrated parents. These words are sometimes said because we either do something childish or behave in a childish way.

Growth is something important to all of us. From the moment we are born we are weighed and measured. Right through infancy parents and doctors monitor our progress either on their records or on the back of the living room door. This is an important factor in our development.

Likewise, our spiritual growth and development is very important but seldom given the same attention. The Bible speaks a lot about spiritual growth and development. "Be not children in understanding but in understanding be men." 1Cor. 14:20 "Be no more children...grow up into Him in all things." (Eph.4:14,15; 1Pet.2:2)   Although growth is the natural result of good nutrition and exercise we should never take it for granted. Quite often something can stunt growth and then we are really concerned.

Paul was concerned that these Colossian Christians would be retarded in their growth and development because of the ideologies of certain errors that were being taught in Colosse. Judaizers and gnostic mystics tried to entangle them with all sorts of teachings about angels, astrology, ceremony and tradition. With pen in hand Paul exhorts them to keep their eye on Christ and to press on with Him.

In the previous chapter we considered these two points:

1. BE SURE A Sense of Affection (2:1-3)
2. BEWARE A Sense of Alarm (2:4,8,16)

We now proceed to look over the shoulder of the Apostle Paul and into the advice he gave those first century saints

3. BECOME! - A SENSE OF AIM (2:6,7)

"Thrift or Drift" is a maxim that the Bank of Scotland used some years ago. They were obviously encouraging people to safeguard against inflation by trying to keep ahead of it. The same maxim may well be applied to the Christian life. "Grow up or drop dead!" Spiritual growth is the best safeguard against slipping into heresy or lethargy. Paul's passion was that the Colossian Christians might grow; therefore, so he gave us a series of metaphors in which he illustrated how we need goals for growth. If we do not thrift we will drift!

(a) A soldier (v.5)

Here is the picture of a soldier. With order and steadfastness he is marching in rank. Such order demands the discipline and obedience of a good soldier. We have been called to be soldiers, and we are under orders to please Him who has chosen us to be soldiers. (2Tim. 2:3,4) Be sure to keep in step with the Commander!

(b) A pilgrim (v.6)

Peter reminds us that we are "strangers and pilgrims." A stranger is a person who is away from home and a pilgrim is a person who is going home. The Christian is both. As we commenced our pilgrimage in the pathway of faith, so we are to continue in a walk of faith. The Gnostics wanted to add something more to Christ. Paul's prayer for these Christians was that as pilgrims they would walk worthy of their Lord. (1:10;4:5) It is interesting how often we are reminded of our "walk." (Eph.5:2,8) Be sure to keep your eyes on your target - home.

(c) A plant (v.7)

The godly are often likened to flourishing plants. A good example of this is the first Psalm where they are portrayed as "a tree planted by the rivers of water, that bringeth forth his

fruit in his season; his leaf also shall not wither; and whatsoever he doeth shall prosper." As a good tree so also a Christian
should be rooted in Christ.

Only as we put our roots down do we know productive
fruit in our lives. (2Kings 19:30) When the roots are firm, then
the fruit will come and the foliage shall be good. It is
important to take care of the soil of our quiet times with God
and our attendance to the things of God. Be sure to keep your
roots in good soil.

(d) A building (v.7)

"...and built up in Him, and established in the faith." Again
this is a common metaphor of the Christian life. (1Cor.3:9)
Christ is our sole and sure foundation. (1Cor.3:11) However,
on the foundation of our faith we are to build with good
materials - not with the wood, hay and stubble of indulgent
and empty works but with the good materials of gold, silver
and precious stones. (Heb. 6:1; 1Cor. 3:12-15)

Someone said, "The biggest room in the world is the room
for improvement." Peter tells us to keep adding to your "faith
virtue; and to virtue knowledge; and to knowledge temperance; and to temperance patience; and to patience godliness;
and to godliness brotherly kindness, and to brotherly kindness charity. For if these things be in you and abound, they
make you that you shall neither be barren nor unfruitful in the
knowledge of our Lord Jesus Christ." (2Pet. 1:5-8) Be sure
you keep building with the right materials.

(e) A student (v.7)

"...as ye have been taught..." Epaphras had taught these
believers the first principles of the Christian faith. (1:7) Paul

prayed that they might be filled with the knowledge of the wisdom of God. Having begun with the spiritual alphabet, they were now into the deeper teachings of Christ. (Heb. 5:11-14) A professor one day said to his class, "If you get this into your heads, you will have it in a nutshell." We need to get the Word of God into our hearts and into our minds so that it resides in us richly. (Col.3:16)

There is a difference between a normal Christian life and a nominal Christian life. Too many Christians live on the level of nominal Christianity. They are undeveloped simply because they are untaught. A. W. Tozer said, "Refuse to be average." Vance Havner said, "Paul speaks of spiritual babes who won't grow up. Some of these 150 - 200 pound church babies keep the pastor busy running around with a milk bottle when they should have been on beefsteak years ago." Be sure to dwell in the Scriptures and let them dwell in you.

(f) A river (v.7)

"Abounding" has the sense of bursting the banks and flowing over. In the Amazon jungles many of the houses are built on stilts. The residents expect the river to flood every year in the rainy season. As the fullness of God fills a Christians life, he should be overflowing in gratitude to God. When a cup is full, any little movement will make it spill over. It will only spill out what is inside. How often when we are upset, we spill out bitterness instead of sweetness.

I remember some years ago driving Dr. Ian Paisley through Belfast. I happened to refer to a brother who had become upset and very bitter. Dr. Paisley said to me, "Victor no matter what happens in God's work, keep sweet." I never forgot those words. Be sure that when you overflow, the sweet floods of gratitude spill out of your life

4. BEHOLD! A SENSE OF ADEQUACY
(2:9-15)

Paul now points the believers to Jesus Christ; "In Him dwelleth all the fullness of the godhead bodily." (2:9) He then links this fullness in Christ to our completeness in Him; "And you are complete in Him." (2:10)

(a) All the Fullness of the Godhead in Him
(v.9)

What a blessed truth for believers assailed by the false doctrines of emanating angels. Jesus Christ eternally is, ever was, and forever will be, in all respects, fully God in all His being and attributes.

The word "fullness" was often used by the Gnostics to express the source from which the emanations of mystical angels came. Paul set forth that there were no emanations from God. It is only in Christ there is the meeting of the heavenly and the earthy, the divine and the human. He who came from God, as God, has returned to God and eternally is God.

(b) All the Completeness of the Christian in
Him.

If the former truth was difficult to grasp, then this is even more so - that we have been made to share in His fullness. He Who is the fullness of God, fills us.

Where we lived in the Amazon, we were almost three thousand miles from the mouth of the mighty river. Dipping a jar into the waters of the Amazon would allow the fullness of the great river to fill the jar. However, my jar could never contain the fullness of the greatest river in the world. Nor could I contain the fullness of diet. Christ, who is the fullness of the godhead, fills my heart, and in Him we have the fullness of God and are complete in Him.

Three times Paul refers to our position as "in Him." Because in Him dwells all fullness, then that fullness is ours by virtue of our position in Christ.

Christ is our Baptism. This speaks of the baptism of death. In Christ we died.

Christ is our Circumcision. This is His death. Earthly circumcision was cutting off the skin. Christ was cut off for us, and through Him we also have been cut off from all of our past failure and debt to the Law.

Christ is our burial. The burial of Christ was the evidence of His death.

Christ is our resurrection. The resurrection of Christ is the heart and hope of the Christian faith.

Christ is our life. Jesus Christ is our life. "It is no longer I that lives, but Christ that liveth in me."

Jesus Christ is sufficient and we are complete in him. No heretic can sing,

"Thou, O Christ art all I want,
More than all in Thee I find."

All that we need is in Jesus Christ. He met all the requirements of the Law and satisfied all the demands of divine justice . As a debt that was paid, so "He nailed to the door the document" - an expression that shows a public declaration that a debt has been cancelled. Our debts to the law have been settled at Christ's expense.

He not only paid our debt, He also spoiled the powers that were against us and openly triumphed over them. Is it any wonder we sing"The Old Account was Settled Long Ago?"

The truth of this is even more emphasized by Paul's use of the present tense, "ye are complete in Him." Nothing can be added to completeness. When a believer is born into the family of God, he is born complete in Christ. If anyone attempts to take our attention away from Christ and our completeness in Him, then beware of that person.

5. BELONG! A SENSE OF ALLEGIANCE (2:16-23)

Again Paul warns the believer of the danger of being hijacked by those who would impose legalism, mysticism, ritualism and stoicism to their faith.

When we are complete in Him, we are like ships rigged and made ready to sail. It is good to remember to whom we belong and under whose command we put. Christ is our Captain. His Word is our chart and the Holy Spirit our compass. He has given us our colours and He will bring us to our desired haven. (Psalm 60:4; 107:30)

8

"HEAVENLY MINDED AND HEAVEN BOUND"

As we enter into chapter three of Colossians, I am reminded of the children of Israel entering Canaan and enjoying all the fruits of "the land flowing with milk and honey." Having crossed over Jordan they sampled the choice grapes of Eschol. How rich and juicy they were. So here also, as we pass from one chapter to another; there flows from the pen of the Apostle Paul some of the most precious vintage of doctrinal and practical truth ever expressed by pen and ink.

"If ye then be risen with Christ..." Paul in his letters often laid the foundation of doctrinal truth, and then on the basis of the truth, indicated the practical implications that flow from it. For an example of this see Ephesians 4:1 and Romans 12:2.

Here in Colossians 3, Paul employs the same principle. Having laid a sure foundation on the basis of our "completeness in Christ," Paul then affirmed that we are risen with Christ,(2:9-12) he now moves to the Christian's conduct in the world.

Initially, there are two things that stagger us as we first enter the chapter. First of all, there is the wonder of the terms Paul uses - "In Christ" and "with Christ." The truth of our union "with Christ" follows the truth of our position "in Christ." Note Paul's use of the prepositions "in" and "with." "Saints in Christ" 1:2 "Faith in Christ" 1:4 "Reconciled in Christ" 1:22 "Redeemed in Christ" 1:14 "Complete in Christ" 2:10

Flowing from our position "in Christ", Paul then changes to our union "with Christ." In our position "in Christ" we focus on our possessions "in Him." In our union "with Christ" we focus on our identification "with Him."

"Died with Christ"	2:20
"Buried with Christ"	2:12
"Quickened with Christ"	2:13
"Raised with Christ."	3:1
"Hid with Christ"	3:3
"Appear with Christ"	3:4

What a comprehensive and indissoluble union we enjoy with our Lord. Did Christ die? Then so did we by our identification with Him . This matter of identification pervades the teaching of Paul throughout the New Testament and should have a practical impact in our lives.

A young lady once wrote, "Yesterday I was worth fifty dollars, but today I am worth millions." She had married a millionaire. So also, the sinner saved by grace is united with Christ and is therefore transformed from spiritual poverty to the amazing place where he is as rich as Christ is. Paul teaches this to the Corinthians in 2 Corinthians 8:9, "For you know the grace of our Lord Jesus Christ, that, though He was rich, yet for your sakes He became poor, that you through His poverty might be made rich."

The other truths that stagger us on entering this chapter are the tenses Paul uses.

Past   "Ye have been raised."

Present   "Your life is hid with Christ."

Future   "Ye shall appear with Him."

How comprehensive is the sweep of all this. The Christian is crucified with Christ; raised from the grave with Christ, hid in God with Christ, and soon we shall appear in glory with Christ. From the grave to glory all the way "with Christ."

1. THE HEAVENLY LIFE WITH CHRIST "RAISED WITH HIM..."

(a) The Miracle of the Heavenly Life "raised"

Every conversion is a spiritual resurrection. (John 5:24,25) "...and shall come into condemnation, but is passed from deaths unto life." There is no other way to new life other than by the miracle of resurrection in your life. Before conversion there was no living. We were dead in trespasses and in sins.

Years ago there was a fine body of Christian men in east Belfast who ran The Coal Men's Mission, adjacent to the Belfast Coal Quay. They were just simply known as "The Coalmen's Testimony Band." As the name suggests, they all were coalmen who had been soundly and gloriously converted by the grace of God. Besides those great meetings at the Coal Men's Mission, "Pop" Stewart, "Wee" Sammy

Spence (sometimes called "Dodger Spence"), Billy Stewart, Tommy Hunsdale, Bob Moffit, Sam Dunlop and many others travelled all over Ulster and beyond testifying of what God had done in their lives. Those days predated what we know now as "the mini-bus" and to see all these burly men, with the exception of "Wee Sammy" climb in and out of small Morris 8 cars and match box Austins, was painful to watch. They nearly needed a shoe horn for the operation.

Ingeniously they hit upon the idea of buying an old hearse. They removed the platform at the rear of the hearse that was used to carry the coffin, and in its place they put seats so that the hearse would carry about ten people. Although the hearse had been converted to a mini-bus, it still looked like a hearse.

Wherever they travelled, people stopped at the approach of the hearse, farmers would respectfully lift their hats thinking that the remains of someone were in transit to their final resting place. However, when the hearse got up close, there were "Wee" Sammy, "Big" Billy, "Pop" Stewart and all the boys as large as life and singing from their hearts. People looked aghast, only to read on the side of the hearse, "PASSED FROM DEATH UNTO LIFE!" At the rear they had their motto, "Heaven via the Cross."

(b) The Means of the Heavenly Life "with Christ"

"Christ being raised from the dead, dieth no more" (Rom.6:9) The source and secret of our new life is the empty tomb and our risen Lord. While the earthly man perishes, yet because He lives we shall live also.

I remember when I studied at the Missionary School of Medicine in London, I went to hear Dr. Martyn Lloyd-Jones at his Bible Study every Friday evening. Every week for almost three months he preached on the phrase "..and believe in thine heart that God had raised Him from the dead." "The Doctor" was at pains to stress that the fundamental truth and evidence of the Christian Gospel is the resurrection of Jesus Christ. The resurrection pre-supposed all truth that predated it and anticipated all purpose and promise that was to follow. The power of the Gospel message is the power of the resurrection. 2. THE HIDDEN LIFE WITH CHRIST "Hid with Christ..." There is a great parallel between these verses and 1John 3:1-4. We are so hid with Christ in God that "it doth not yet appear what we shall be." When a thing is hidden, we immediately think of it being hidden in darkness. When we think of the unbeliever, we are reminded that he is in spiritual blindness. However, as any motorist will be aware, it is possible for a thing to be hidden in the light of the sun or the lights of an oncoming car. I suggest that the believer is hidden by the brightness of God.

This hiding place "with Christ in God" is secure. The Psalmist constantly addressed God as his Refuge, his hiding place in trouble. (Psalm 46:1)

The famous "Sanci" diamond was sent from a French nobleman to Henry IV. The messenger who carried the diamond was ambushed by thieves who left the man for dead, but they could not find the diamond. When the authorities found the body they opened the abdomen only to find that the messenger had hidden the diamond in his stomach. We are so hidden in Christ. No robber shall ever touch us there. (John 10:28,29; Col.2:3)

A tyrant threatened to kill a believer for his faith. To this the believer replied, "You may touch my body, but my life is hid with Christ in God." Two Ulster men leaned over a fence, each nibbling at a piece of grass. One looked up to the sky, and seeing a silver jet gleaming in the sun at a distance with the jet stream following, said to his friend, "I wouldn't like to be up there in that thing." The other looked up and replied, "I wouldn't like to be up there without it." It is a terrible thing to be without Christ.

3. THE HOPEFUL LIFE WITH CHRIST "YE SHALL ALSO APPEAR"

"To Appear" is to make manifest what has been hidden. As we are raised with Christ, and as we are hidden with Christ, so shall we be manifested with Christ. The late Pastor Willie Mullen of Lurgan used to say, "If the unsaved really knew that Christians are the aristocracy of heaven, they would tip their hats at us." When Jesus Christ appears we will then be manifested with Him. (1 Pet.1 :3 Eph.1:13)

An unbeliever asked a believer, "Do you think that when you get to heaven the Lord will know you and you will know Him?" The Christian replied, "Of that I have no doubt, but what puzzles me is that I'll hardly know myself!" The Christian has a glorious future when Christ shall transform us to be like Him. (Phil.3:20,21)

4. THE HOLY LIFE IN CHRIST "SEEK...SET..."

Because these truths are real facts, then flowing from them should be a heavenly mind set. Setting our affections on things above involves our minds and our hearts.

(a) "Seek with your heart..." (3:1)

Seek heaven. Set your affections on the highest things. Jesus Christ reminded us that where the treasure is, there shall the heart will be also. On 1st September, 1985, Robert Ballard discovered the hull of the great "Titanic" 350 miles off the coast of Newfoundland and lying at a depth of two miles on the ocean floor. This is what he said about his quest for the sunken ship. "My first direct view of the "Titanic" lasted for less than two minutes, but the stark sight of her immense black hull towering above the ocean floor will remain forever ingrained in my memory. My life long dream was to find the great ship, and during the past 13 years the quest for her has dominated my life." Robert Ballard lived day and night for something that was hidden in the depths. God asks us to live for that which is above.

(b) "Set your mind..." (3:2)

Think heaven. What we set our minds on determines what we seek in life. The battle for the mind rages strongly today. Peter reminds us that we are to "arm ourselves with the same mind" as was that of our Saviour. Paul also reminds us that the transformed mind is the mind that is conformed to the mind of Christ. "Let this mind be in you which was also in Christ Jesus."

An insight into the mind of Christ is given to us by the writer to the Hebrews when he admonishes the Christian to run the race, "Looking unto Jesus the Author and Finisher of our faith; Who for the joy that was set before Him endured the cross, despising the shame, and is set down at the right hand of the throne of God." (Heb. 12:2) Our Lord throughout His life not only had the cross in mind but also, beyond the cross, the joy of His accomplished work and return to the Father.

When, during World War II, our soldiers fought in France and Germany, although they were on foreign soil their hearts and minds were on the homeland. Many of their songs were of the ones they loved back home. It was the thought of returning home that spurred them on to victory. What a picture of the Christian. We are going home, our treasure is there, our Saviour is there, and for many of us, our loved ones are there. Keep heaven on your mind.

9

"HE IS MY EVERYTHING"

COLOSSIANS 3:4-14

One thing we have noted in this book of Colossians is that Jesus Christ, according to the theology of the Apostle Paul, is everything. Paul sets Christ forth as our Deliverer, Redeemer, Creator, Living Head, the exact Image of diet; and Paul also states that in Him all the fullness of the Godhead dwells bodily. The Apostle further adds "And you are complete in Him." There is little wonder, therefore, that when Paul speaks of the community of believers, he declares, "Christ is all and in all"(3:11) That is the theme of this epistle; "Christ is all in all."

All this was against a background where gnostics, judaizers and Greek philosophers were seeking to infiltrate the church and destroy the foundations of the Christian faith. Paul, with pen in hand and prayer on his heart, sought to combat such infiltration. He addresses himself to basically two matters.

First, there is the matter of what we believe about Christ and then there is the matter of how we behave as Christians. There should be a correlation between both of these.

In Paul's writings, theology was always related to biology. For Paul, doctrine demands duty, creed determines our conduct and facts are followed by acts. This is borne out by Paul's use of "therefore" in Romans 12:1, "I beseech you therefore, brethren, by the mercies of God..." Ephesians 4:1; "I therefore, the prisoner of the Lord, beseech you that you walk worthy of the vocation wherewith ye are called." It is again evidenced here in Colossians 3:5; "Mortify therefore your members which are upon the earth;..." When we apply the theme of Colossians to our lives we come up with the following; because "Christ is all and in all," it will therefore be seen in:

1. DENYING THE OLD LIFE. 3:5-9

(a) Put to death the works of the flesh. 5-7

"Mortify therefore your members that are upon the earth; fornication, uncleanness..." This is radical language from Paul, but it is consistent with what our Lord Jesus taught, "And if thy right eye offend thee , pluck it out and cast it from thee." To mortify is to put to death, to kill, to starve to death. Many years ago the practice was in England, and still is in some Eastern countries to this day, that a thief had a hand cut off as punishment for his crime. But cutting off the hand did not solve the problem of the heart. It is in the heart that we need surgery. Paul catalogues some things we need to put to death.

IMMORALITY - *(Porneia)* This takes the whole spectrum of immoral sexual relationships: fornication, adultery, homosexuality, incest, sexual relations with animals. The Gospel swept clean all the filthy habits of the pagan world. Chastity was alien to the Greeks, and the Gospel brought a radical change to the community of believers.

If we gratify and feed the lusts of the flesh or allow pornography to infiltrate our minds and lives, these things will then lead us to immorality. Rather than gratify the lusts of the flesh, we are to mortify the desires of the flesh, put them to death, starve them.

IMPURITY - This is wider than physical immorality. It is the indecency that provokes the imagination, effects speech and determines attitudes. It is what we call a filthy mind and tongue.

Inscribed in stone above the door of the home of BBC in London, Bush House, are the words of Lord Reith, one of the founding father of the famous corporation. "To Almighty God. This shrine of the arts, music and literature is dedicated by the first governors in the year of our Lord 1931, John Reith being Director General. It is their prayer that good seed sown will produce a good harvest, that every thing offensive to decency and hostile to peace will be expelled, and that the nation will incline its ear to those things which are lovely, pure and of good report, and thus pursue the path of wisdom and virtue." We certainly have moved a long way from those first ideals. Today the same corporation poisons the minds of the nation with a diet of anti-Christian programmes and often vulgar and blasphemous language not to mention the pornography shown on our television screens.

LUST - The shameful emotion that leads to sexual impurity. (1 Thess.4:5; Rom. 1:26) Desires lead to deeds, and appetite leads to action. Starve them!

COVETOUSNESS - This is pure greed, always wanting more than it ought to have. This is the person who is never satisfied but has a craving for more things. He becomes intoxicated with things. This is idolatry. (Heb.13:5,6)

When Christ is all and in all there is no room for a sensual life style. The above sins are prominent in society today and bring the anger of God on our nation. Sadly, even some who profess the name of Christ live on the fringe of such sin. (Prov.6:27; Mat.5:29)

(b) Put away the Words of the Flesh. (8,9)

Paul had been warning about the sensual sins of the flesh; now he comes to the social sins. Sometimes we tend to think these sins are more acceptable and may be tolerated, but in the life of a believer it is worse than in the non-Christian.

ANGER - This is the growing, seething, inner-anger like steam in a kettle that is building up pressure.

RAGE - This is the sudden outburst of temper by the boiling over of anger.

MALICE - Here is a malignant attitude that plans evil and delights when misery falls on its victim.

SLANDER - There is a degeneration in this list. What has been as metal heated in the fire of rage now is expressed a s poison arrows of the tongue. (4:6)

FILTHY LANGUAGE - Left unchecked, slander follows on to filthy language - foul, obscene and abusive speech. LIES Remember that Satan is the "Father of lies." When we lie, we side with the Devil against the "Spirit of truth ." (Psm 141:3) These are the things we are to "put down" and to "put off."

2. DISPLAYING THE NEW LIFE. (3:10-14)

Reminding us that we have been raised with Christ (3:1,9,10), Paul admonishes that we are to take off the grave clothes of t he old life and put on our new wardrobe of heavenly attire. We are new creatures, chosen of God, holy and dearly beloved, and God has tailored beautiful new clothes for us. Paul writes, "Keep putting these garments on."

COMPASSION - Tenderness of heart. The ancient world was merciless. Christianity brought compassion to the world. (Mat.9:36) It still does. **KINDNESS** This word has behind it wine which has matured and lost its harshness. It has become mellow. Kindness does not happen naturally. It is listed as a fruit of the Spirit. (Gal.5:22)

HUMILITY - The Greeks gave no virtue for humility. They had no word for this quality that would not suggest weakness . They had contempt for humility. Jesus Christ took a word of contempt and dignified it. (Mat.11:30; Phil.2:8) In an age of arrogance and pea-cock-like attitudes, humility is a rare quality. Remember, only the drooping wheat stalks have heavy grain! God hates a proud look. Humility is not what your estimation of yourself might or might not be, it is thinking of others first before yourself. Humility is not defensive of itself but is protective of others. Humility is a rare quality indeed! I heard of an pastor who won a medal for being the most humble pastor in his denomination. The medal was taken away from him two weeks later when he insisted on wearing the medal!'

GENTLENESS - Meekness can be misunderstood to be weakness. Not so. "I am meek," said Jesus Christ. Gentleness is strength under control. "Thy gentleness has made me great." (Psalm.18:35; Numbers 12:3) Moses was the meekest of men, but he was never a weak man.

PATIENCE - This is long temper as in a metal- the ability to stand up under pressure. Bearing up in the face of insult or injury.

FORBEARING - We are told to "forbear one another." - Put up with each other. None of us is perfect. But God is at work in us. All of us need to learn to put up with each other. We are to bear and forbear.

The kindest and the happiest pair
Will find occasion to forbear;
And something everyday they live,
To pity, and perhaps forgive.

FORGIVING - This follows on from forbearance. If we are not perfect then we all need forgiveness and need to forgive each other. "Forgive us as we have been forgiven." In relation to how much we have been forgiven, ours is a smaller role to for give those who wrong us.

LOVE - This is the final garment. It what we might call "the overall." It is as if when all the garments are on, we now need to secure them all in place with a belt. That belt is love. This is the crowning grace above graces. All the other graces are aspects and expressions of love. Without love all the former qualities are in vain.

Because you are dead; therefore, put to death the works of the flesh. (3:5)

Because you are raised; therefore, put on the new man. (3:12)

3. DIRECTING THE PERSONAL LIFE (3:15-17)

4. DELIGHTING THE DOMESTIC LIFE. (3:18-21)

5. DISTINGUISHING THE BUSINESS LIFE. (3:22-4:1)

10

"MY HEART IS HIS HOME!"

COLOSSIANS 3:15-17

In the last chapter we looked at the new clothes for a new creature. This is not an unfamiliar picture throughout the Scriptures. In Gen. 3:7 we read that when Adam and Eve sinned against God, they covered themselves with fig leaves. These garments were natural but absolutely insufficient. In Gen. 3:21 God took away the fig leaves and provided garments from slain animals to cover the nakedness of our first parents.

Likewise, in Zech. 3:3,4, we find Joshua the High Priest, likened to a "brand plucked from the burning." The High Priest was clothed with filthy garments. The angel of the Lord said "take away the filthy garments...I will clothe thee with a change of raiment."

It is this change of raiment Paul encourages these Colossians to pursue. As new creatures in Christ we are to destroy the old life and display the new life and then let God direct our personal lives. We have been looking at the heavenly wardrobe which God has given us for everyday use, and there are a few more garments for us to wear.

1. THE PEACE OF CHRIST REIGNING OVER US. (3:15)

Someone has said that peace is the smile of God reflected on the soul of the believer. See the various aspects of this peace in the following:

(a) The confidence of this Peace.

"The peace of God" is more accurately "the peace of Christ." Some hours before Christ died He said, "Peace I leave with you; my peace I give unto you." (John 14:27). This is the peace that He both made for us and gave to us. We first experience this peace when we come to know Christ and find peace with God in reconciliation and the peace of God in our hearts. (Rom.5:1). This peace does not depend on the tranquility of circumstances on the outside. Rather, in spite of the adversity of circumstances, His peace gives us an inner calm. It is peace because we are pardoned and now we enjoy His presence. Paul reminds the Philippians that "the peace of God shall garrison your hearts and minds.... and the God of peace shall be with you." Phil 4:7,9

Peace with God - good;
Peace of God - better;
God of Peace - best.

(b) The control of this Peace.

"Let the peace of God rule in your heart," The words "let" and "rule" are one word in the Greek. "Let the peace of Christ function as an umpire in your hearts." In Greek society the word referred to the function of one who took it on himself to decide what was right or wrong in a contest. I'm sure that was not an easy role.

Missionaries to the Chol Indians in Mexico sought a word for peace. The translators found a word that meant "a quiet heart." That is what peace is, a heart that rests in God. Remember Peter on the night before his execution? His quiet heart enabled him to sleep. That Christian is greatly blessed where the peace of God reigns in his life.

It has often been my experience when faced with a difficult decision, after prayer, counsel and thought were all given and the decision then made, peace flooded my heart. That was the assuring token that I had taken the right decision. However, it has also been my experience that when I have made a wrong decision my heart was in turmoil until things were put right. Well did the psalmist pray, "Unite my heart to fear Thy Name." The heart that is divided does not have that inner calm. Only when our will is aligned to His will does His peace keep us.

The Christian who lives in disobedience loses his peace. When we stray we lose that peace. As the referee tells us when the footballer is "offside," so God's peace is the referee to indicate when we go astray. However, as we walk in the will of God, His peace is the assurance of God's presence and consent.

(c) The communion of this Peace.

"Called to one body..." When God's peace reigns in our hearts, there is harmony in the body. It is interesting to note that this peace reigns in "hearts" among the "members" of the same body. This teaches us that peace should reign amongst the relationships of the Lord's people. How much difficulty, division and misery we would avoid if we let the peace of God rule in our hearts and in our church fellowships.

When we live in disobedience, we lose that peace, and the Church body loses that peace. We owe it to God to be at peace, we owe it to ourselves to be at peace and we owe it to the Church, the body of Christ, to be at peace.

In the winter two porcupines huddled together to try and keep warm. Their quills kept pricking each other. They decided to separate. Apart they nearly froze to death so they needed to get together again but the more they got together the more they needled each other! How true this is in the life of many churches where believers "needle" each other.

2. THE WORD OF CHRIST RESIDING IN US (3:16)

"Let the Word of Christ be at home - find rich hospitality - in your hearts." Paul had already reminded them that no place, nor welcome should be given to false teachers or philosophers.

(a) Receiving the Word of God.

In English we don't make a distinction between the "you" of second person singular and second person plural. "You" covers both singular and plural. Colloquially in Northern Ireland we differentiate with "you" and "youse" or "yous'ns"! Grammatically it is wrong, but it makes the difference. It is important to note that Paul spoke collectively to all the believers at Colosse when he said, "Let the Word of Christ dwell in YOU." There should be a rich and wide reception of the Word of God in our lives and in all the Church. (1Thess.2:13)

It is also interesting to note the parallel passage in Ephesians 5:18-6:9. In Ephesians the emphasis is on being filled with the Spirit; whereas here in Colossians the emphasis is on being filled with the Scriptures. The outcome is still the same. Being filled with the Spirit and filled with the Scriptures will effect our church life, home life and secular life.

(b) Results of the Word of God.

Flowing out of a life or a church where the Word of God has its proper place, is a sense of worship and joy. John Phillips in his commentary on Ephesians reminds us that to be filled with the Spirit is to be thrilled with song. This is also true of the life which knows the parallel filling of the Spirit and the Word. Singing is a telltale sign of the richly residing Word. One book, the Bible, leads to another book, the hymn book. Paul classifies the songs prompted by the Holy Spirit. Psalms suggested musical accompaniment. Hymns were praises unto God. Songs were general admonition and exhortation.

The early church which "continued steadfastly in the apostles' doctrine and fellowship, and in breaking of bread, and in prayers," also continued in "praising God and having favour with all the people. And the Lord added to the church daily such as should be saved." (Acts. 2:42-47) Remember Paul and Silas singing in prison (Acts 16:25) Singing and great songs were a feature of great revivals in all countries throughout the history of the Church. Read the great songs of the church that were born in revival times and compare them with many of today's songs and you will find the difference is the content of the Word of God. Perhaps the paucity of Scriptural preaching in our churches is the reason for so many unscriptural songs that are being sung. The songs we sing are to be sung with grace in our hearts and gratitude to the Lord.

3. THE NAME OF CHRIST RESPONDING FOR US. (3:17)

"Whatsoever you do in word or in deed, do all in the name of the Lord Jesus." Again we need to enter into the atmosphere and ethos of the believers in Colosse to know the impact of these words. Among the members of the Colossian Church were slaves who may have felt that they had been unjustly treated. Paul inspires them to excellence and quality by the greatest motivation - "do all in the name of the Lord Jesus."

(a) The Actions we Take.

What could be more comprehensive than this exhortation? "Word or deed" take s in everything in life. Everything we say and everything we do is to be done "in the name of the Lord Jesus." What a safeguard on behaviour! Is our word our bond? Are we dependable? Is our work our testimony? If we admit anything into our lives that is not done and cannot be done in the name of Jesus, it is wrong.

(b) The Authority we Use.

What's in a name? My father and uncle Davey where well known soccer referees. Sometimes when I got into a spot of trouble and had to give my name to a policeman I was asked if I was any relation to Davey Maxwell. How often his name saved my skin! A name represents the character, reputation and authority of a person. We use our own names to authorize our bank cheques. Jesus Christ is the reason and authority behind the actions we take and the words we speak.

(c) The Attitude we Adopt .

"Giving thanks unto the Father." We are back to the garment of praise which should adorn our lives.

4. THE PRAISE OF CHRIST RADIATING THROUGH US. (3:15-17)

Throughout this letter, as through all the letters of the apostle, we find that he abounds in praise unto God. It radiates through the testimony Paul gives here. He associates Christ's peace with praise (v.15), he allies Christ's Word with worship (v.16), and Christ's Name is related to his thanksgiving (v.17).

I remember visiting a young man, Raymond McKibben, in prison. Raymond had received 369 years prison sentence, if all his penalties were to run consecutively. Prior to his arrest he had experienced times of deep conviction of sin, and the on very night of his arrest he had trusted Christ as Saviour. His growth in grace was remarkable. On this visit I asked him if he had a word that I could take to the friends who prayed for him at Templemore Hall. After a few minutes he opened his Bible at Isaiah 61:3 and read these words, "He will appoint... a garment of praise for the spirit of heaviness." He said, "Victor, in this prison there is a lot of heaviness and depression. God has taught me to cover over my heaviness by deliberately putting on a garment of praise every day." He then pointed to Psalm 147:1, "Praise the Lord: ....for it is pleasant, and praise is comely." Raymond then said, "Isn't praise a beautiful garment to wear everyday."

Full buckets always overflow. When we are filled with His peace, His Word and His Name, we will overflow with His praise.

11

"WHAT HAPPENS WHEN GODLINESS COMES HOME"

COLOSSIANS 3:18-4:1

A little girl came home from play school one day with eyes wide open began to recount to her Mummy the story she had just heard for the first time. It was the story of Cinderella. When she got to the end of the story, and Cinderella was finally found by Prince Charming, the little girl said, "And mummy do you know what happened next?" The mother gave the traditional end to the story, "Yes , they both lived happily ever after." "No, no," said the little girl, "they got married mummy!" The little girl in her innocence expressed what is a sad fact of our modern world. Getting married and living happily ever after are not necessarily one and the same thing.

In our modern society families are in trouble. We also must admit that even Christian families are not exempt. One of the major problems is that couples, and sometimes Christian couples, have moved away from God's original design.

Many will point to the fact that times have changed! They sure have. Some people choose marriage like they would choose a record. They like one side of the record but are not too keen on the other side. After a while both sides are boring so they get rid of the record. Discarding of partners and disregarding solemn marriage vows is getting to be like that. How different from the pattern God first intended.

Peter Marshall, author of "Mr. Jones Meets the Master," wrote, "Marriage is not the federation of two sovereign states.

It is a union, domestic, social, spiritual and physical. It is the fusion of two hearts, the union of two lives, the coming together of two tributaries, which, after being joined in marriage, will flow in the same channel, in the same direction, carrying the same burden of responsibility and obligation."

Paul here in Colossians puts marriage in the theological and spiritual context. Constantly through his letters Paul shows us that godliness in our personal life should also effect the domestic life. It matters to your church life and your Christian witness how you behave at home. (1Tim. 3:4; Tit. 2:4; 1Pet. 3:1-9) On that basis Paul gives a series of commands which he had also given in his letter to the Ephesians which was written about the same time. These commands have to do with the home - the Christian home.

1. WIVES, HUSBANDS AND HEADSHIP. (3:18,19)

These verses should be viewed with the parallel instructions in Ephesians 5:22-33 and 1 Peter 3:1-7. One is a commentary on the other. It doesn't take a degree in Greek to know that Paul is giving commands about roles, not in any order of superiority or inferiority but rather to show the need for balance.

Stuart Briscoe asks, "Can you remember the name of the famous, one-armed violinist? Also, do you remember the famous American, one-winged eagle? I doubt that you do, for neither ever existed. It is as impossible to play the violin with one arm as for an eagle to fly with one wing." The same is true in marriage. Wives have a role to play that is different from a husband's but not, in any way, inferior. Husbands have a role to play that is, in no way, superior. They are complimentary roles which are related to unique patterns given to us by our Lord and Creator.

(a) Wives and their Loyal Submission. (v.18)

Paul addresses ladies first. Paul is a friend to all ladies. What he was teaching was completely revolutionary. We must remember the context of the times in which Paul was writing.

Under Jewish law a woman was a "thing". She was the possession of her husband, just as much as his house or his sheep. She had no legal rights whatsoever. The husband could divorce her almost at will. In Greek society a respectable woman lived a life of entire seclusion. She didn't even join the men folk for meals. There was demanded from her a complete servitude and loyalty, but the husband was free to have as many relationships as he wanted, and that without any stigma. When Paul speaks of "submission," immediately some will recoil thinking of a slavish, unpaid submission to a tyrant as an inferior is to his superior. Nothing could be further from the truth. The submission of our Lord Jesus to His Father was not from inferiority to the Father. He is co-equal with the Father. Rather, it was loyal co-operation and loving devotion to the Father and His will - each in His own role. That is the submission that is spoken of here. It is a submission that is supportive of the husband "as is fitting in the Lord."

The godly wife might well ask, "Lord, how can I show my love for you in the role you have given me?" The answer comes, "You show it by your submissive and supportive heart toward your husband." The husband is the head, but you may play the role of the neck to give support and help give direction to your husband.

Now the Bible is not silent on a lot of the thorny problems that arise in marriage. While speaking of the role of the wife, Peter enlarges on this and underlines three practical guide lines for the role of the wife. (1Pet. 3:1-6)

The Wife's Actions. (3:1)

The scene is familiar. The husband does not accept your faith, he may even be hostile to it. Peter reminds the godly wife that her behaviour is the greatest sermon she can preach. The unbelieving husband is not won by the tracts she puts in his pocket or verses pinned to his pillow - rather by him observing her actions as though he were a spectator of a game.

The Wife's Appearance. (3:2-4)

It is important to note here that Peter is not against the adorning of a wife. On the contrary, he encourages it. Some people abuse these verses in "having a go" at what a woman should wear and how she should appear. They major on not having the hair plaited nor permed and not wearing any jewelry. The difficulty with that is, if we follow it through as a prohibition, Peter goes on to prohibit the "putting on of apparel." What Peter says about the hair, gold and apparel is not by way of prohibiting it. He is stressing that external attraction can never be a substitute for internal quality. The emphasis should not be on the outer woman but on the inner woman. Peter is not down on the outward appearance, but it must be balanced with the inner quality.

The Wife's Attitude. (3:4-6)

"The hidden person of the heart" sums up the attitude that women should have and Peter reminds ladies it is the "gentle and quiet spirit which is precious in God's sight." What lovely words. Peter holds Sarah forth as an example. She was supportive of Abraham and had quiet confidence in their future.

(b) Husbands and Their Loving Sacrifice. (3:19)

Paul now gives the counterpart injunction for husbands to "love their wives." This was even more radical for men than for women. Colossians were used to submission, but no man was interested in loving his own wife with this "agape" love. It just was not done. However, for the Christian husband who asks, "Lord how can I be the sort of man you want me to be as a husband?" The Lord's reply is, "By your limitless love for your wife, you show to the world and Me the sort of love you have for Me."

Folded into these instructions are two great questions that every partner should ask. The wife must ask, "Do I love my husband enough to live for him?" The husband must come to terms with the role God has given him and ask, "Do I love my wife enough to die for her?" This is what Paul had in mind as he viewed the husband's love as a parallel to the love of Christ for the Church. See. Eph. 5:25-33; 1Pet.3:7 The Scriptures give three practical guidelines to husbands. Live with your wife. (1 Pet. 3:7) This does not mean to just be under the same roof as her, but rather "closely aligned to her, completely at home with her in companionship and togetherness."

Love your wife. (Eph.5:25)

"...as Christ loved the church." This is not an erotic love nor even a friendship love. This is a love that sacrifices for her. Man is selfish by nature. He must sacrifice and give unselfish love to her. Such love sustains and is sympathetic to her.

Lead your wife. (1 Tim.3:4,5)

"He is able to manage well his house." Some tend to think that the husband's role is his external job at the place of employment, and the woman runs the home. Not so, the husband is responsible before God for the leadership of the home.

Here then are two radical calls. One to wives: submission and support. The other to husbands: to love as Christ loves. These should not be read in isolation. Remember the one armed violinist?

Paul continues to apply the truth in a practical way to the home life of the believer.

2. CHILDREN, FATHERS AND RELATIONSHIP. (3:20,21)

(a) Children and Their Obedience. (3:20)

(b) Fathers and Their Obligations (3:21)

3. SERVANTS, MASTERS AND THEIR WORKMANSHIP. (22-4:1)

(a) Servants and their work. (3:22-25)

(b) Masters and their wages. (4:1)

We shall look at these in the following chapters.

12

"CHIPS OF THE OLD BLOCK"

COLOSSIANS 3:20,21

A little boy one day stood in a railway station and watched a great train which was on exhibition. The boy said, "Daddy ask the man how much the train costs." The father did just that, and when he was told that it cost a considerable sum he remarked, "My, that cost just as much as our new church." Just then the boy pointed to the engine and said, "Yes, Daddy, but at least the engine works."

What is the use of studying and preaching the Word of God if we are not able to make it work and prove it in our daily lives - not just in church, but in the home and out of doors? Paul was insisting that Christianity does work. The responsibilities of parenthood were on the heart and mind of the apostle as he wrote to the Colossians and the Ephesians (6:1-4). Our Christian life is brought into our homes. It should touch our personal life, our domestic life, our business life, our recreational life, our social life and every other part.

We live in a security minded age. Just over these recent days we have been reminded of horrific robberies where thieves have broken into homes and cars to steal goods and large and small sums of money. All of us are vulnerable. Even church buildings are targeted .

In this climate, can you imagine the manager of the local jewellers asking you to store all his stock of precious stones and jewellery in your home over the next two weeks while he goes on holiday? I think that you would rightly decline and tell him to find a more secure place.

Such a responsibility is light when compared to the weight of the treasure that God has placed in the homes of all parents. The Bible says, "What shall it profit a man if he gain the whole world and lose his own soul." If you would place all the treasures of the jeweller in one room and your boy or girl in another room, remember that the child is of far greater value than the jewels. If we would tremble at the thought of losing the jewellers fortune, how much more should we tremble if we should lose our children?

In the matter of domestic life we already touched on the initial partnership of husband and wives. The atmosphere they create in the home by their sacrificial love and loyal support, should follow on to build good relationships with their children. Children are a joy and delight but also a great responsibility. It is as if God was saying to us as was said to Jocabed, "Take this child home and nurse it for Me and I will give thee wages." (Exodus 2:9)

I preface my remarks here by pointing out that parents are not perfect. All of us are wiser by looking back and realizing the mistakes we have made and what we might have done differently. However, let us look at God's plan for parent/child relationship. It is more again of the sort of complimentary roles as in husband/wife relationship.

1. CHILDREN AND THEIR RESPECT FOR PARENTS. (3:20)

(a) Obey your parents.

"Children obey your parents in all things". Obedience for many is a hard word to swallow, and when it is demanded, it often provokes a reaction and a battle of wills. Someone has said, "Conflict comes in a home where there is a will and a won't."

We all admit there is a lack of respect for authority in school, in Sunday school and in society. However, all of these problems come back to where authority must be taught and respected, and that is in the home. A child's first encounter with authority is in the home. We were all born rebels and early in life the child's voice of rebellion and selfishness may be heard. Sadly, instead of parents exercising discipline and creating respect, many of them just want peace and quiet at the expense of training the children in what is right.

Obedience is something we all must learn. We learn by speed limits, by security alarms, by fire guards, by danger signs, etc. It is a normal human experience. However, in the home it is a fact, that we too often, and at the peril of losing the respect of our children, ignore and disregard our Christian responsibility to teach our children by discipline. It is the biblical way to train a child.

The word "obey" is a compound word of "listen - under." "Children, listen under your parents in all things." Children should learn to listen and to be under tuition to do what is right. "In all things" is a very broad term. However, given the context of a Christian home where parents love the Lord and love their children, then what the parents may ask the children to do should be consistent with their Christian commitment. Where wrong things are commanded then we must "obey God rather than man." As Christians we should respect and honour our parents in our obedience to them.

(b) Honour your parents.

The word "children" should be looked at. We tend to think of a child as an infant or an adolescent in the growing years when guidance is needed. The Hebrew word for "old" carries the thought of a "bearded one." For a man maturity often corresponds in time to when he can grow a beard. There comes a time when we are no longer under parental responsibility , and we are then taught to " honour your father and your mother."

The words that were etched by the very finger of God on the tablets of stone and Paul commands are: "Honour thy father and thy mother that it might be well for thee." As we mature to adulthood it remains our responsibility to honour our parents and to make sure no parent suffers want in the necessities of life. (Mk. 7:9-13; 1Tim 5:3,8) It has been said, "We love our equals and honour our superiors". However, where there is true love for parents there will be honour and respect for those parents as an expression of our love for them. As Christians we respect our parents by honouring them.

(c) Please the Lord.

Obedience "in all things." This is the measure of our obedience. "For this is well pleasing in His sight." This is the motive for our obedience. We can have no higher motive than this. As Christians we respect our parents because we seek to please the Lord.

2. PARENTS AND THEIR RESPONSIBILITY FOR CHILDREN. (3:21)

The word "fathers" can also read "parents." A paper entitled "A Scientist Looks at Love," reported a survey carried out on 239 institutionalized children in a Latin American country. This very revealing survey was carried out over a period of five years. The children were confined to two different environments. Both of these were equal in housing, food, hygiene, etc. They differ ed in just one factor - the amount of loving attention provided. The contrast in results was dramatic. In the first where love and care were shown, the children from three months onward showed normal to advanced development. In the second, where there was no show of love, the emotionally starved children were retarded in their development. After two years they were not able to speak, not able to walk, and not able to feed themselves. In this second home the mortality rate was 37%, while at the first home they did not lose one child.

Although it is sad to use little children for a blatant statistical survey, yet one thing is clear, love is essential for human development and a healthy and happy home. The absence of love or the wrong type of love in a home only produces heart-breaking results. Proverbs 15:17 states, "Better is a dinner of herbs where love is, than a stalled ox and hatred therewith."

(a) Parents are to Exhort Their Children - teaching them.

George Washington is greatly honoured as the "Father of the United States." He was very successful as a soldier and leader, but he was a failure as a father. He confessed, "I am able to govern people but not able to govern my boys."

Paul tells the Ephesians we are to bring our children up in the "nurture and admonition of the Lord." The word "nurture" speaks of chastening and disciplining. The book of Proverbs was written as the counsel and teaching of a father to his son. Forty times it says "son" or "my son." For example, "Chasten thy son while there is hope and let not thy soul spare his crying." (Proverbs 19:18) "The rod and reproof give wisdom: but a child left to himself brings his mother shame." (Proverbs 29:15) "Spare the rod and you will spoil the child." (Proverbs 13:24). The dilemma of teaching the child is how to shape his will while protecting his spirit. We are not to exasperate our children. We must discipline but not abuse, shape but not crush the children. We are to teach him. (Proverbs. 1:10-16; 3:11,12; 5:1-5; 23:19-21 ; 10:4,5).

(b) Parents are to be Examples to Their Children. - training them.

Training children is taught by Solomon when he says, "Train up a child in the way he should go: and when he is old, he will not depart from it." (Prov. 22:6). The word "to train" is a horticultural term in which you bend a tree or the stem of a plant to make it grow in the direction you want it to go. It is also the picture of putting a bit and bridle on a horse to train him. So it is we are to bend and steer our children in "the nurture and admonition of the Lord." Admonition is even more important than nurture. In nurture we teach a child, but in admonition we train a child. Example is always more important than exhortation.

(c) Parents are to Encourage Their Children - trusting them.

Life is not easy for children, and they need all the encouragement they can get. If they do not get it from their parents, where will they get it from? Remember a farmer may try to stamp out the weeds, but that is not his first concern. His main purpose is to grow a harvest, and to encourage the crops. In our homes we are not to run a regime. We want to encourage our children to prove Christianity at home.

A little boy's first Bible
Is the greatest thrill he's known.
There's a sweet, unique excitement
In a Bible all his own.

And yet my heart is smitten
As this touching sight I see.
Has his reverence for that Bible
Depended much on me?

As I see him with his Bible,
I bow my head and pray,
"May he always love that Bible
The way he does today."

Then I hear a voice within me
Speak in solemn words and true
"How he cherishes that Bible
Will depend a lot on you."

Author Unknown

13

"WORSHIP WHILE YOU WORK"

COLOSSIANS 3:22-4:1

The charge is sometimes made that Christians are too heavenly minded to be of any earthly use. That certainly was not the attitude of the Apostle Paul. Colossians chapter three begins in the heavenlies and with our position in Christ. The progression of the chapter brings that heavenly citizenship right down to earth and to the personal life, the domestic life and to the business life.

We already said it takes two wings to fly, two arms to play a violin and two people to play tennis. So it is also important to remember that Paul couched all his instructions about the home and work in the balance of mutuality: wives and husbands in partnership; children and parents in relationship; servants and masters and their workmanship. None of these relationships are with people who are remote or distant from us. They are all close to us. Paul was concerned about the Christian witness to people in our homes, in our street and in our work. There is a challenge to our lives in what is said of our Lord Jesus, "The Word was made flesh and dwelt among us and we beheld His glory." Jesus manifested His presence wherever he went in those three years of ministry. When someone is resident in a place we generally know about it. So if Christ has taken up residence in us, then surely His presence should be evident in how we relate to our wives, to our children, to our work. We must take Him into every area of our lives.

Having dealt with the home, Paul now addresses the work place. Consider the following Scriptures: "He becometh poor that dealeth with a slack hand: but the hand of the diligent maketh rich. He that gathereth in summer is a wise son: but he that sleepeth in harvest is a son that causeth shame." (Prov. 10:4,5) "And ye that study to be quiet and do your own business, and to work with your own hands as we commanded you. That ye walk honestly toward them that are without and that ye have lack of nothing." (1Thess.4:11,12). Paul loved hard and honest work and considered it to be a holy, healthy and happy pursuit. Paul Carruth said, "Some people remind us of blisters - they don't show up until after the work is done."

Hard work may sound alien to some who conclude that hard work came as a result of the fall of Adam in the Garden of Eden. Work is not a consequence of sin. Adam was made for work and worked before he sinned. As soon as God created Adam, He gave him a job to do . "And the Lord God took the man, and put him into the garden of Eden to dress it and to keep it" (Genesis 2:15). It was sin that made work a burden. The absence of work often leads to sin. It is reported that bees imported to Barbados worked feverishly preparing for winter. When they found there was no winter to work for, they turned their activity to stinging people. Many of society's problems today are related to so much unemployment The sting of our community today is that many cannot find work, while others do not want to work.

Paul's counsel to the Colossians on the matter of work may have been accompanied by a certain amount of tension for several reasons. First, we note he took more time to speak to slaves and masters than to husbands and wives. The possible reason for this is that one of the messengers who delivered the letter was Onesimus, a runaway slave who had been reconciled to his master Philemon.

Furthermore, Paul's letter was not only written against a background of a particular case in Colosse, but also in the environment of extensive slavery in the Roman Empire. It is generally acknowledged that there were in excess of sixty million slaves in the Roman Empire - more than one half of the population. Slaves did everything. Manual work was considered to be below the dignity of a Roman citizen. Except in a few cases, the relationship between masters and slaves was not a happy one. Roman tradition classified slaves as mere tools to be used during their best years and to be discarded when their use had expired. This meant that a master had the power of the life and death of a slave in his hands. If a slave ran away and was caught, he would have been put to death or have had the letter "F" branded on his forehead reminding everyone that he had been a "Fugitivus."

In the context of this environment, you can imagine the tensions there might have been in the church, where slaves and masters had come to the Saviour. Paul proclaimed in Galatians 3:28, "There is neither Jew nor Greek, bond nor free, male nor female, for you are all one in Christ." Christian equality was a sensitive problem to wrestle with in that primitive church. Think of the strained relations between Onesimus and Philemon. Paul had instructions for them both.

It was not Paul's intention to fight against slavery, nor did he sanction it. Here in the United Kingdom and in the U.S.A., slavery was only abolished in the last century. Paul's crusade was not the social reform of the Roman Empire but the transforming of individual lives through the Gospel in that Empire. Such evangelism and church planting ministry eventually led to the overthrow of the Empire. The preaching of Wesley and Whitefield was not aimed at the abolition of slavery and child labour, but it resulted in it.

Although the language used is that of slaves and masters, and it was couched against the culture of the ancient world, this portion of Scripture remains valid, and Paul's instructions are appropriate and applicable to us and our employment at the end of the twentieth century. The term "servant" applies to employees and "masters" to employers today.

1. THE DEVOTION OF A CHRISTIAN EMPLOYEE. (3:22-25)

"Slaves obey your masters in all things." That was and is a tall order. A slave listening must have thought, "Whose side is Paul on anyway?" The Christian slave owed complete obedience to his master as a testimony of his devotion to his Lord. If a Christian slave had a Christian master, he was not to take advantage of him. The Christian worker should be more diligent at his job than the non-Christian.

Paul's injunction to Christian slaves was that they must:

(a) Work Conscientiously in Singleness of Heart. (3:22)

Paul coins two words here to show how the Christian should work. They were to work "not with eye service" - not just when the eye is on you. I think we all know what that is like. Often a boss has to watch his workers so that he can get the best out of them. A factory put up a suggestion box to improve working conditions. The first suggestion was that the foreman no longer wear rubber heels on his shoes. They wanted to hear him coming! That should not be the case with Christians. A Christian should be a person who can be relied on to work whether he is being watched or not. God is always watching.

They were to work "in singleness of heart, reverencing the Lord," or "With all of your heart, as worship to the Lord." Everything God asks us to do for Him, He expects us to do it with all our heart. That should put a different emphasis on our work. A single heart and a sincere heart are necessary for proper service to the Lord.

(b) Work Consistently as a Servant of Christ. (3:23)

The commands here are strong - "obey...submit." However, they should be read in view of the Christian's highest motive "as unto Christ,...ye serve the Lord Christ." The recording company R.C.A. have adopted the old fashioned symbol that had the dog sitting at the gramophone listening. We called it "The Masters Voice." The question we must ask is, "Who is my Master?" Our Master is not just the boss or foreman, He is our Lord in heaven.

We used to receive envelopes that had at the top of them these letters "O.H.M.S." - on Her Majesty's Service. The Christian should not be working as a man pleaser. His work is a gift from God and as a servant of Christ he seeks to serve Him. He is on His Majesty's service. Nearly two hundred years ago the editors of "The Times" had great a embarrassment. Every copy they produced had many typographical errors. Finally, they told the compositors and printing staff that the first copy of the press would be sent to the King. Immediately the quality improved because they were prompted by greater motivation.

H. Ironside tells the story of an English tutor who was employed by the royal house of France to teach a young prince to speak English. The princely pupil was difficult to handle for he was proud and haughty. The teacher was at his wits end for he didn't know what to do. He hit on an idea. One morning as the prince came in the tutor pinned on him a purple rosette, saying, "This is the royal colour, and as you wear it I want you to remember you are the Crown Prince of France, and you must behave as such." Wearing the colours of his country made the prince behave in a more responsible way. We should also bear the colours of the King of Kings. "Thou hast given a banner to them that fear Thee, that it may be displayed because of the truth." (Psalm 60:4)

(c) Work as Committed in Service to Christ. (3:24)

All through these latter verses we have repeated the use of the word "master." Parallel to "master" are the names of "God" and "the Lord." It is as if Paul was over-writing, "You have a master in heaven." Often when I preach I try to imagine that the Lord is sitting in the front pew listening to what I am saying and how I am saying it. I wonder, have I done my best for Jesus? In your mind picture Jesus Christ with you at your work. Such thoughts and meditations would soon solve many of our problems.

Three things to say about our service to Christ: We are responsible to the Father in our Service to God. We are not just working on a material plane but on a spiritual plane. We are to work whole heartily - not half heartily. We are not just working for the temporal but for the eternal. A Christian worker said one day to a missionary n the service of the Lord, "Who would do it for a fiver a week?" If that is the attitude, then they are not serving the Lord.

We are recognized by the Father in our service to God.

We are not men pleasers, but rather, all we do is seen of our heavenly Father and He will reward us openly. (Mat.6:4)

We are rewarded by the Father for our service to God.

Becoming a Christian costs you nothing, but being a Christian costs everything. He has promised that there is nothing that we sacrifice for Him, but that He will give us one hundred-fold in this life and glory in that which is to come.

2. THE DUTY OF A CHRISTIAN EMPLOYER. (4:1)

In these verses Paul is speaking to Christian masters who have a maturity in the Lord. There are several things that are important for the Master to consider:

(a) The Work of the Employee.
(b) The Welfare of the Employee.
(c) The Witness of the Employer.

Ina Orr, the wife of my missionary colleague Fred Orr, died in Brazil just two months after arriving in the country. On her tombstone are written these words from John 17:4: "I have glorified Thee on earth having finished the work which thou gavest me to do."

14

"PRAYER CELLS - A VIEW FROM THE PRISON"

COLOSSIANS 4:2-4

The study of the ancient world is fascinating. Ancient Egypt was known for its pyramids and tombs; ancient Greece was famous for its philosophers and temples, but ancient Rome was noted for its laws and roads. Roman roads once covered a total of 53,000 miles extending from Rome to the extremes of the empire all over Europe and Asia Minor. The engineering marvels of the network of Roman roads is an enduring reminder of their greatness.

The early church has also left us a pattern of roads that they opened. They are not for commerce or temples, but roads for God's truth - God's roads. Instead of stemming from Rome, the highway of the Gospel rolled out of Jerusalem carrying the Good News of the Gospel of Christ to the most distant corners of the world. The vehicles God used to accomplish this Mission were those of men who went out praying and preaching.

The Apostle majors on these tools of service as he nears the end of his letter to the Colossians.

1. COMMUNING WITH THE LORD. (4:2)

None of us like being told what to do. Right since we were children we always questioned orders given to us. When Paul gave these instructions to the Colossians, they might have felt rebuked about the matter of prayer. Prayer is the obvious duty of the Christian. However, it is also true that prayer is the most difficult discipline of the Christian life. Paul had been teaching them about the home and work, but now he reminds them they are also to keep their mind on heavenly things. Keep on looking up. The Apostle describes three aspects of praying which should be cultivated.

(a) Faithful Praying.

One of the most common sins of God's people is that of prayerlessness. No doubt this has been the case throughout the centuries. Is it not for this very same reason that the Bible constantly reminds us of our need to pray? "Men ought always to pray and not to faint," said the Lord Jesus. "Pray without ceasing," writes the Apostle Paul. It is true, "Prayer is the Christian's vital breath." No one who neglects this spiritual exercise can have a happy and triumphant Christian life. The soul flourishes only in an atmosphere of prayer.

Paul admonished the Christian Colossians to pray continually - pray without quitting. Perhaps you say, "That is impossible. I have to work and do a hundred other things. How can I pray continually?" No one was more busy than our Lord or the apostle Paul. Neither of them spent their lives in a cloistered room on their knees. They were public people. Continual prayer is living in an attitude of prayer and keeping in touch with God. Too soon we give up. Satan will do his evil utmost to hinder us. The flesh will grow weary, we get tired and lazy and sometimes discouraged. Do not give up. Prayer is a devotion we need to express, a discipline we need to exercise, a dynamic we need to experience. Continue in prayer.

(b) Watchful Praying.

Compare Nehemiah 4:9 with 1 Peter 5:8. We need to be awake and alert in our praying. Before you pray, watch for things that need to be prayed for and make sure you actually do pray for them. Watch while you pray so that you come reverently, confidently and yet submissively. Watch after you pray to see how God answers your prayers. In response to prayer God replies in one of the following ways:

1. No. God says I love you to much to give you this. This is a denial.

2. No, not now. This is a delay.

3. Yes, you may have it. This is our desire.

4. Yes, and here is more. This is God's delight.

(c) Thankful Praying.

A legend is told of two angels sent to earth, each with a separate mission. The first was to gather up all the petitions of men and women. The other angel was sent to collect their thanksgivings. The first angel found petitions everywhere and returned to heaven with a load of them on his back and other bundles in each hand. The second angel had a difficult time. He searched diligently, and when he returned to heaven, he had but a handful of thanksgivings.

It is only a legend, but it underlines an accurate truth - we are long on demands and loud in our complaints, but often we are lacking in our thanksgivings. Paul gave the Colossians an example of gratitude. (1:3; 1:12; 2:7; 3:17) Paul was always sure to wear the garment of praise as everyday clothing. It was woven into the fabric of his life.

This gratitude not only cultivates confidence but also contentment. Two girls went out to gather grapes. One was happy to find grapes; the other was unhappy because the grape they found had stones in them. Two ladies in a garden noticed a bush. One was unhappy because it had thorns; the other was happy because it had roses. We ought to positively develop and cultivate the habit of thanksgiving to God in all things. (Phil. 4:6) Thanksgiving exalts the Lord, expels the gloom and encourages other Christians.

2. COMMUNICATING WITH THE WORLD (4:3,4)

Paul not only prayed for the saints and encouraged prayer for the church, he was not ashamed to request the prayers of the other Christians for himself. He requested prayer constantly. (Eph.6:18; 2Thess.3:1) Spurgeon had his "power-house prayer meeting" while he preached. What Paul requested gives us an insight into the man.

(a) The Opportunity

"God would open unto us a door of utterance." Paul had not been looking for an open door out of prison. I think if we had been in prison we would have seen it as an obstacle to our witness and would have been looking for a way out. Paul saw the prison as an opportunity, and he wanted to make the most of every opportunity. Someone said, "A pessimist sees a problem in every opportunity whereas an optimist sees an opportunity in every problem." Paul was that sort of optimist.

Paul was faithful to his calling, but he had an open mind on how to reach people. When you read his life, you find it was unpredictable. You would not know what he might do next, where he would go next or what he would say next. Well did he say to the Corinthians, "I make myself all things to all men that by all means I might save some."

What a contrast to our stuffy, dull, rigid and habitual service which we render to God. In church we often rank the novel alongside the immoral and the criminal, and are just as strong against any thing new. We tend to be suspect of anything that is not traditional. If our traditions become a hindrance, then there is something wrong with our traditions. We need to disturb our stereotype approach if we would break the ice and really reach out to people. Pray that God will stir our hearts and cause us to anticipate the opportunities He gives us. Paul was looking for opportunities even in the prison in Rome. (Phil.1:12-14)

(b) The Obligation.

"A door unto us ... as I ought to speak..." There is hidden in this request a sense of individual and collective responsibility. Collective responsibility in that he speaks of all of "us" which includes all the fellow workers he refers to throughout the rest of the chapter. God has a work for us to do. Individual responsibility in that God had a part for Paul to play. Each of us has an inescapable responsibility to play our part and fulfil our obligations to God.

(c) The Opposition.

"I am in bonds." Every time the Lord opens a door of opportunity to a church or an individual, the Devil always raises opposition. Paul said to the Corinthians, "For a great door and effectual is open unto me and there are many adversaries ." (1 Corintians 16:6) If you are determined to reach people for Jesus Christ, be sure you will be opposed. Principalities and powers are against us. (Eph. 6:12;) I heard of an officer who said, "Men we are surrounded. Don't let one of the enemy escape."

Each year in London the Lord Mayor's Banquet is held. All the dignitaries are there with their chains of office. They wear them with pride and honour. The British Prime Minister, as is customary, will take the opportunity in his after dinner speech to address the nation and let the mysteries of his policies be known.

At the other end of the scale tonight some young terrorists are wearing chains also. They wear them with humiliation and some with shame because of their crimes. May I just remind you of this scene with Paul. As a prisoner he also had a chain. It was meant to be a chain of humiliation. He bore it with honour. He took the opportunity given as a prisoner to make known the mystery of the Kingdom of God, as an ambassador in bonds. To Timothy he wrote, "I am suffering even to the point of being chained like a criminal, but the Word of God is not bound." (2Timothy 2:9) Paul was no "Chocolate Soldier."

15

"RELATIONSHIP AND FELLOWSHIP"

COLOSSIANS 4:7-18

Sometimes it is said of a Christian worker, "He is very good, but nobody could work with him." Dr. Sangsgter told a story of an organist giving a recital in a village church where the organ was pumped by hand. After each piece played there was loud applause, and the organist would then announce what he was going to play next. Behind the curtain was a simple man pumping the bellows that gave wind to the organ, and he was getting increasingly irate at the conceit of the organist taking all the praise. Finally, the man could take it no longer. When the organist announced his next rendition in the same conceited manner and then sat at the keyboard to play, there was no sound from the organ. The man at the pump had stopped working! He poked his head out from behind a curtain and shouted at the organist, "Let's have a little bit of 'we' in it instead of 'me' all the time."

One of the things I have learned over the years is that Christian service is never a solitary effort. Many others have their part to play in any work undertaken for the Master. There are others who went before us. My wife and I, for many years, have been members of Acre Gospel Mission. We are grateful to God for Mr. & Mrs. Willie McComb and Miss Mollie Harvey, the founders of the work in Brazil, and all our fellow workers who went before us and raised up the testimony and maintained it through the years. We thank God for every remembrance of them. Currently I am pastoring Templemore Hall in Belfast, and we are grateful for those who work alongside us in church. We are workers together with God. One sows and another reaps, but God gives the increase. There will be those who follow us, and we are confident that the Lord will preserve the witness and testimony of this work.

Paul never lost sight of the fact that there were others in the battle besides him. We all like to surround ourselves with portraits of people who have had input into our lives. At home and in my study we keep photos of people for whom we pray and others of people who have been a blessing to us. In the book of Acts there are at least one hundred different names of people associated with Paul and his work. He names sixteen different friends in the last chapter to the Romans, and here in the last chapter of Colossians h e alludes to another ten people. The inclusion of these names suggests to us some of the co-operation fellowship involved in doing God's work.

1. TYCHICUS THE MESSENGER. (4:7,8)

It was said of Winston Churchill that he was a master of giving thumb nail sketches of people. He could sum their character up in a few words. So also with Paul. He did not use a great volume of words in speaking about his friends, but what he said spoke volumes.

Tychicus whose name means "fortunate," is mentioned five times in five different New Testament books. (Acts 20:4;

Eph. 6:21; 2 Tim. 4:12; and Titus 3:12) However, each reference to him is always consistent that he was a faithful brother in Christ. He had been a constant companion of Paul's, and through thick and thin Paul had proved him to be a loyal friend. Paul gave Tychicus a good character reference.

(a) A Beloved Brother.

It seems that this man had captivated Paul's heart and those of his colleagues and he won a place in their affections. There was something winsome about him. Undoubtedly, some of the troubles through which they had passed had bound them together in bonds of Christian love. It is important to employ our experience to make us better and not bitter.

(b) A Faithful Minister.

Tychicus was not only known for his love for the saints, but also his faithfulness to God and His cause.

There is no indication that he was known for any preaching gift or any prominent place in the church or Colossian society. His ministry was that of being a messenger for Paul. In the U.K. there are people who are known as the Queen's messengers. These are reliable men who are chosen for their loyalty to the Crown. They carry diplomatic messages to ambassadors or heads of governments. Reliability is their virtue. Paul had obviously proven Tychicus to be a reliable friend.

Someone said, "The greatest ability in the world is dependability." Such was Tychicus. As a messenger, he was sent to deliver Paul 's letters to the Church in Ephesus, to the Church in Colosse, to a slave owner named Philemon and also to the Church in Laodacia. He also delivered letters to Titus. He played the role of a message boy for the Apostle.

There are no records of any great works that Tychicus did or that deserved mention in Luke's writings. We should not despise the day of small things. This man was a servant who did his work to the Lord. There is greatness in the smallest things that are done for the Lord. Small things done for the Lord are only small in time, but they are great in eternity. Jesus Christ Himself assumed the place of a Servant, and He exalted service to a place of dignity and divinity.

(c) Fellow Servant.

The Apostle showed that the messenger and the writer were yoked together in the same work. "My hand may write this letter, but his feet run the errand. We are both serving the same Lord in different capacities."

2. ONESIMUS THE MEMBER (4:9)

What thoughts might have been in Colosse when Onesimus' name was mentioned? He was known in Colosse, and this worked both to his advantage and his disadvantage. No man is a hero in his own home town. He had been known as a slave and a sinner. Now he was to be recognized as a saint and a servant.

(a) He was known for his Failure.

It was matter of abiding shame to Onesimus that there had been a dark side to his life. He had been a bad man. He had taken advantage of his master, stolen from him and had ran off to Ephesus and Rome. "Like the moon, every man has a dark side that is never seen."

(b) He was known for his Forgiveness.

It might have seemed incredible to those in Colosse that the grace of God had reached and changed Onesimus. His life was so transformed that where once he had robbed, he made restitution. Once he had been ungrateful and scheming, but now he was giving unselfish service to those whom he had once offended. How wonderful is the grace of the Lord Jesus!

(c) He was known for his Faithfulness.

Onesimus' name simply means "useful." This name had been a contradiction in Onesimus' life. While he had lived in sin and for sin, his life had been useless. However, now that he had known the Saviour for only a short time, his life was proving to be useful. So changed was this man's life that Paul noted two outstanding qualities - his love and his faithfulness.

While Onesimus may have been unique, yet he is typical of many who have been so completely transformed by the grace of God. Such people are living adverts and witnesses of the grace of God.

3. ARISTARCHUS AND THE MISSIONARIES (4:10)

Paul also associates Marcus and Jesus, which was called Justus, with Aristarchus. These three were Jews but were also associated with Gentile believers - all made one in Christ. We know that Aristarchus had been with Paul since the days in Ephesus. (Acts 19:29) His life reflected what true companionship in the Lord's work meant.

(a) They were Fellow Preachers.

"Fellow workers in the Kingdom of God." The object of

going with the Gospel was to do the sowing of the good seed of the Word of God. That was their mission in life.

(b) They were Fellow Prisoners.

Aristarchus had landed in jail with Paul. Not only did they speak together, they had learned to suffer together. When hard times came, Aristarchus did not shrink from the prison for the sake of the Gospel. There are too many fair weather friends who forsake their commitments when trouble or allurement comes.

Aristarchus was a refreshing contrast to Demas who is mentioned in verse fourteen. Very soon he was allured by his love for the present world and forsook Paul. Also note in verse ten what a difference had taken place in John Mark who had deserted Paul and Barnabas in the middle of their evangelistic trip.

(c) The Fellow Helpers.

"These only are my fellow labourers unto the Kingdom of God, which have been a comfort unto me." (4:11) The word "comfort" means "encouraging one." As the word "encourage" simply means to "put courage into," so the word "comfort" (com = with, fort = strength) means "with strength." These companions carried each other's burdens and put strength into each other. You do not have to be a greatly gifted person to be an encourager but if you are an encourager, that is a great gift.

4. EPAPHRAS THE MINISTER (4:12)

Not all God's heroes have familiar names. My Sunday School teacher was a quiet man who did not raise his voice too much nor got too excited even though he had a class of boisterous boys. He had a passion to teach boys the Scriptures, and although we did not appreciate it, at least four of the boys out of his class went into the ministry or to the mission field.

(a) Epaphras was a man of purpose - "A servant of Christ."

He probably founded the work in Colosse. He was a man with a target: to plant Christ's name in towns of the Lycus Valley.

(b) He was a man of passion - "Who labours fervently."

The two words that underline his passion are "zeal" and "fervency." There is a sense of wrestling in this word. These two words speak of sweat and hard work.

(c) He was a man of prayer - "labours...in prayer."

The secret of the success of his work was his prayer life. He was unceasing and unselfish in his prayers.

Many of us find it hard to remember names. One way to cultivate a good memory for people is to show interest in them and major on some outstanding feature. Paul was interested in people. He not only remembered their names but their qualities also. In mentioning his friends by name in his letter, he indicated how much he appreciated their worth and value, and esteemed the part they played.

16

"OUR WILL AND HIS WILL"

COLOSSIANS 4:12-18

The conflict and resulting tragedies in Northern Ireland are often referred to as the clash of two different traditions with two different aspirations. Perhaps a more simple and basic way to speak of this unhappy turmoil is to speak of the clash of two wills, or as someone said, "Where there are two wills there is either a war or a lawsuit."

Every conflict, be it a domestic row in the home, a union dispute in the work place, civil unrest in a nation or war between nations , is basically a conflict of human wills. My will against your will.

If you stop to analyze all of this, you will soon discover that these contentions between human wills are often brought about because of a higher conflict - the conflict between the human will and God's will.

In this final study we want to focus on a man for whom Paul had the highest commendation. In opening the letter to these Colossians he mentions Epaphras. This man was a

Colossian and possibly was the founder of the churches in Colosse, Laodacia and Heirapolis. Paul referred to him as "a servant of Christ." Throughout the letter he qualifies Epaphras' role as a servant:

A fellow Servant of Christ	1:7
A faithful Servant of Christ	1:7
A fruitful Servant of Christ	1:6-8
A fervent Servant of Christ	4:12

The fervency of Epaphras to which Paul alluded was expressed in his prayers for the Church at Colosse. The burden and essence of that prayer was that the Christians in Colosse would "stand perfect and complete in all the will of God." He was praying that instead of their experience of the will of God being a battle of two wills, there might be a blending of those wills resulting in the Christian proving what is the good, perfect and acceptable will of God.

In his excellent book "Decision Making and the Will of God," Gary Friesen pictures two circles. One circle represents God's will, and the other represents our self will. While they are apart they are contrary the one to the other. When you move one circle to be covered by the other, self will to be conformed and uniform to God's will; they are no longer in opposition. The battle of wills has given way to blending of wills. That is what Epaphras is praying for these Christians in Colosse.

1. THE PROBLEM OF DISCERNMENT AND THE WILL OF GOD

Few Christians will deny that at times there is a problem in understanding God's will. Often it seems cloaked in a fog of mystery and misunderstanding. There is nothing more frustrating than trying to pick our own course through life under a cloud of doubt and uncertainty. Decision making never comes easily. Just this week I heard the funny story of a man who was given a job sorting potatoes. He was told to sort potatoes into three categories: small potatoes, medium sized potatoes and large potatoes. After three days he told his boss that he could not take the stress of his job. The startled boss was surprised to hear there was stress in sorting potatoes and asked what was giving him stress. To this the potatoes sorter said, "I can't stick the stress of constantly making decisions." Some decisions come easily while others seem to be so crucial.

On the other hand, there is nothing more satisfying than to be assured that you are living according to the will of God.

As a young Christian I was introduced to Navigators, an organization set to give counsel and a plan for growth for new Christians. Dawson Trotman was the founder of the Navigators. I still remember the day I was shocked to hear of the "untimely" death of this gifted and greatly effective young man. He had been to Schroon Lake, New York and had decided to have one last run on the water skis. In fact, it turned out to be his final run, for it ended in a tragic accident in which Dawson was drowned. His friends were shattered.

It is said that when they phoned Dawson's wife to tell her the sad news, they just said, "Lila, he's gone." Although stunned she quietly quoted in return Psalm. 115:3, "But our God is in the heavens: he hath done whatsoever He hath pleased."

At the outset of the Apostle's letter to the Colossians he prayed that these new converts "might be filled with a knowledge of God's will in all wisdom and spiritual understanding.." (1:9) We might well ask, "Why is it important to understand God's will?" Paul gives us the answer as he continues, "...that ye might walk worthy of the Lord unto all pleasing." An understanding of God's will is not to satisfy our curiosity, but God gives us an understanding of His will so that we might undertake to do His will. Our Lord taught us all to pray "Thy will be done on earth as it is in heaven."

In an attempt to clear up some common misunderstandings about the will of God, the following analysis will give us a rule of thumb.

(a) God's sovereign will.

God's sovereign will is understood to be all of God's control over all of His creation. Listen to the Scriptures, "He doeth according to His will in the army of heaven and among the inhabitants of the earth..." (Daniel 4:35) See also, Proverbs 21:1,2: "The kings heart is in the hand of the Lord, as the rivers of water; He turneth it withersoever He will. Every way of man is right sin his own eyes; but the Lord pondereth the hearts." Revelation 4:11: "Thou art worthy, O Lord, to receive glory and honour and power; for Thou hast created all things, and for thy pleasure they are and were created." Ephesians 1:11: "...the purpose of Him who worketh all things after the counsel of His own will." The Scriptures conclusively teach us that God the Creator is in total control of all His creation. Augustine said, "Nothing, therefore, happens unless the Omnipotent wills it to happen: He either permits it to happen, or He brings it about Himself."

(b) God's moral will.

God's moral will is understood to be all God's commands to all His creatures. God is holy and He demands holiness. The Bible is replete with statements indicating God demanding conformity to His holiness. 1 Thessalonians 4:3: "For this is the will of God, even your sanctification..." 5:18: "In everything give thanks: for this is the will of God in Christ Jesus concerning you." 1 Timothy 2:3,4: "... God our Saviour; Who will have all men to be saved and come to a knowledge of the truth." Charles Hodge reminds us, "All moral obligation resolves itself into the obligation of conformity to the will of God."

(c) God's individual will.

Elsewhere Paul speaks of the will of God in personal and individual terms. Romans 12:1,2: "I beseech ye therefore, by the mercies of God, that ye present your bodies...that ye may prove what that good, and acceptable, and perfect will of God." (See also Ephesians 2:10; Psalm 32:8.) God has a plan for your life and for my life. God has a blue print for each of us.

When we speak of the moral will of God, we are thinking about character, but when we think of God's individual will, we are thinking more about our calling. The will of God should dominate the Christian's character, regulate the Christian's conduct and formulate the Christian's career.

It is also true that God has given to us a free will to exercise our volition within the limits of the ability He gives us. Hence, the Christian, because he is joined to Jesus Christ, is able to know, prove and do God's will.

When Paul speaks of "knowing" the will of God, this conveys the idea of discerning God's will. This discernment is spirit taught and comes with maturity. A life-long relationship with the Lord gives you an understanding of His will. My wife Audrey and I are two separate people, but the Lord has made us one unit. After almost thirty years of marriage I think I know and understand her likes and dislikes - at least at times I'm right! Love and relationship know what others do not know. In such a relationship spouses know and anticipate the thoughts and desires of the other. The Christian who has accompanied the Lord for many years gets to know, to discern God's ways in his life.

2. THE POWER FOR ENABLEMENT TO DO THE WILL OF GOD

At the beginning of the letter Paul prayed that they might know God's will. Now he reminds the same Colossians that Epaphras also is praying for them that they "might stand perfect in all the will of God." One prayer is related to the other. The first prayer is a bout discerning God's will, while the second is about doing God's will. It should be remembered that God works in us not just to will, but also to do His will. (Philippians 2:13)

To stand "perfect and complete in all the will of God" is to stand firm and assured. Doing God's will is relevant to every day living. Paul had been speaking to the Colossians about practical living at home and at work.(Col. 3:18-4:1) He now shows them it is possible to prove God's strength to do God's will in every circumstance -- as masters and as slaves, as husbands and as wives, as fat hers and as children. Elsewhere Paul writes, "I can do all things through Christ which strengthens me." Philippians 4:13;

Is it true that the Christian "can do all things?" There are many things Christians cannot do and other things they should not do, but God gives the Christian the strength to do all God wants him to do.

I remember Dr. Vernon McGee illustrated this in the following way. A train is well able to travel at speed and accomplish what it is built to do. However, if you take a train and put it downtown in a city to travel on a highway, it would be cumbersome and useless. It is only useful as long as it stays on the tracks. The train then can do all that it should do and all it was built to do. When we are on the tracks of God's will, He gives us the strength to do all He purposes for us. Remember Gideon of old. When he hesitated to obey God's command, God said to him, "Go in this thy might,...have not I sent thee?" (Judges 6:14) Our sufficiency to do God's will comes from our confidence in His sufficiency in us. By pouring in His power, God enables us to do His will and accept any circumstance.

3. THE PRAYER FOR FULFILLMENT OF THE WILL OF GOD

It is by prayer that we find grace and strength to do the will of God. The greatest service we can render to the church or to a brother in Christ is to pray for the will of God to be done in their lives.

Epaphras prayed that they may be steadfast in character. They needed to stand for God in Colosse. Epaphras prayed that they might be mature in experience. The word "perfect" means to be fully grown.

4. THE PERIL OF DERAILMENT FROM THE WILL OF GOD.

In Col. 4:14 "Demas" is a name that stands as a beacon to us. Later Paul wrote, "Demas has forsaken me having loved this present world." (2 Timothy 4:10) He had become derailed from the will of God. What happened to this man that diverted him from God's purpose? Was it incomplete surrender to God's will? Was it some person whom he loved more than the will of God? Whatever happened, he strayed and therefore was rendered useless.

As a young lad I remember being challenged about God's will for my life. A party of us had gone to Portstewart on the north Antrim coast, for a day in July. After some swimming in what was known as the "Herring Pond", I got into difficulties trying to help a non-swimmer. I was sure I was drowning as I sank several times and my lungs were quickly filling with water. Somehow, I made it to the rocks where I held on for a moment. Just then passersby who had seen us in difficulty, threw out the life belt. They then dragged me to shore where Dr. Love of the Crescent Church in Belfast, administered artificial respiration. I was wrapped in blankets and rushed to nearby Coleraine Hospital.

In the hospital I was humbled at how God had miraculously spared my life. I was a Christian and in prayer thanked God for his preservation. However, I was also greatly challenged that God had preserved my life for a purpose. In that hospital ward, as best I knew how, I handed my life over to God for His will in my life. "Anything Lord, any place Lord, any time Lord, at any price Lord." It was then I understood God's call on my life that would lead to the Amazon in Brazil. But that's another story.

My stubborn will at last has yielded;
I would be Thine, and Thine alone;
And this the prayer my lips are bringing,
Lord let in me Thy will be done

Shut in with Thee, O Lord, for ever,
My wayward feet no more to roam;
What power from these my soul can sever?
The centre of God's will my home.

Sweet will of God, still draw me closer,
Till I am wholly lost in Thee